THE HISTORY OF SANTA CLAUS

The Traditions and Origins of Santa
as Practiced Around the World

by

Tammy Hammond

Dedication

As I have worked on this book, many wonderful Christmas memories were rekindled. Memories of the excitement in my children's eyes and voices as Santa was anticipated, once again delivered smiles to my face and heart. Now, as their children are growing, I am able to enjoy another generation of Santa traditions shared.

I want to dedicate this book to them… Andy, Amanda, Anna, and Alex… thank you for being the greatest gifts a mother could ever hope for.

To the moon and back…

Mom

Contents

INTRODUCTION

As far back as I can remember, I anxiously looked forward to the magical Christmas season arriving. It was the holiday that lasted longer than a single day. The colors, the music, and the smiles were everywhere, and somehow people seemed kinder and happier than they were the rest of the year.

Then there was Christmas Eve, with hushed stories of reindeer sightings as well as the all-out effort to stay awake and sneak a peek at Santa. Somehow we always missed him, but the cookies and milk were gone the next morning, and we were content to believe that Santa had been the one to eat our humble offerings.

More than four decades of Christmas came and went, and I enjoyed watching my own children find the same magic I had experienced. Then, in a totally unexpected way, I found myself once again immersed in Christmas traditions and Santa Claus, this time with a much different perspective. In 2004, a very talented local artist, Loretta Miller, unveiled a collection of life-sized Santas she had designed and hand-crafted. They were incredibly detailed, and each possessed a personality of its own as she had designed them to be "Santas From Around The World." In an effort to stimulate holiday shopping traffic in my hometown of Great Bend, Kansas, Loretta's Santas, which had been featured on national television, were displayed festively in downtown stores. Over time, the effort became less and less organized, and the beautiful Santas became largely-neglected treasures stored in building after building as they were donated from one organization to another.

My acquaintance with the Santas began when we displayed one in my downtown business location. As interest in them dwindled each year, I became increasingly concerned about how we could share these treasures with more people and while giving the Santas a full-time home. A couple more years passed and then, unexpectedly, the perfect building located on the downtown courthouse square became available, one that could properly showcase the entire Santa collection. I purchased the building and renovated it into a winter wonderland of sorts, creating a permanent home for the Santas, where they are now beautifully displayed in environments similar to those of the countries they represent. It's here that you can tour the world through the eyes of Santa.

I began looking for ways to best share the interesting information and stories I was finding as I researched each of Loretta's creations. Finally, I chose to write a series of books, the first of which you're holding in your hands. It is devoted exclusively to the history of Santa Claus. As I researched this world-famous figure, I found that Santa's history had a great deal more depth than I had anticipated. Had there ever been a real Santa Claus? If so, how had the myth of Santa—a man who delivers presents to the world every Christmas Eve—become so popular? Most of all, because the collection I display represents numerous versions of Santa that reflect how he is portrayed in countries around the world, I wanted to write a book explaining how this fabled figure is interpreted in history, custom, and actual practice across the globe.

What follows in this book, is a comprehensive history of who Santa is, what he does, and how he is seen differently in those countries that honor the season of Christmas (and even in a few that don't). He goes by various names, delivers presents by different means, and has numerous helpers and companions (not all of whom are kindly, beneficent characters). In fact, the location of his permanent dwelling is in debate in many cultures, and even here in the United States, the tradition of Santa includes such topics as Mrs. Claus, reindeer, Rudolph, elves, and so much more.

I hope you will enjoy this book and that it inspires you, as I myself have been, to share the magic that Santa represents across the globe.

Tammy Hammond

PART ONE
THE EVOLUTION OF SANTA CLAUS

CHAPTER ONE
The Santa We Know Today

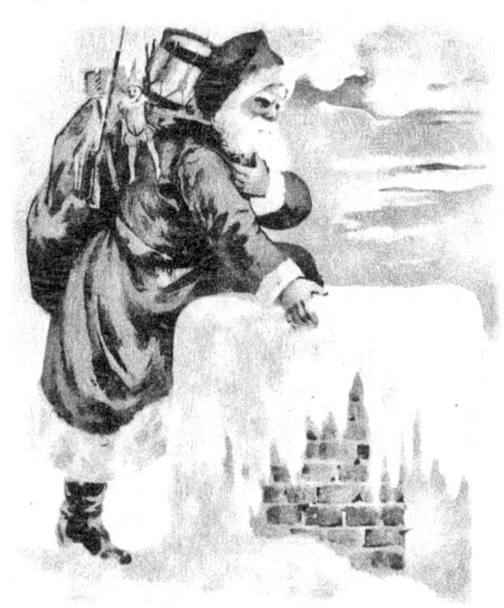

This is Jolly Old Saint Nick carrying the sack of toys from his sleigh. He's plump and is wearing the red furry suit known to the entire world. This is the image that most children dream about on Christmas Eve, and it's still magical!

It would probably be hard to find anyone in the world who has not at least heard of the man called Santa Claus. He goes by many names, both in the United States and abroad: Santa Claus, Father Christmas, Saint Nick, Saint Nicholas, Kris Kringle, and many others that derive from differences in language as well as who he is perceived to be and what he does. To understand the legend of Santa better, let's start with the basics.

In America and Europe (in most of Western Civilization, really), Santa is a jolly fat man who lives at the North Pole, where he has a workshop manned with elves who help him make toys year-round for the children of the world, at least those who are thought to have been nice rather than naughty. He lives there with his wife, Mrs. Claus, who is generally portrayed in art and stories as a somewhat elderly and kind woman who is a bit overweight and wears a bonnet on her head as she takes care of her husband, making him cookies, tea, and small cakes. She is often seen sitting and knitting, usually mending Santa's clothing while he reclines in a rocking chair and smokes a pipe. He is dressed in his traditional red pants but often wears a white, cotton, long-sleeve shirt and suspenders.

Santa is a man who is always in good spirits, and both traditional pictures of the man as well as folk art that goes back for centuries portrays him as having rosy cheeks, a long white beard, and a twinkle in his eye (traits that the Coca-Cola Bottling Company has capitalized on for nearly a century). When fully clothed in his "work outfit," he is seen in red trousers and a thick, red, fur coat that has white fur collars and cuffs. He wears tall black boots, and on top of long, flowing white hair, he wears a red cap (it too has white piping) that falls about his shoulders, ending in a white pom.

But why does this character even exist? The legend of Santa Claus is both extraordinary and supernatural even though most people are acquainted with his duties. On Christmas Eve, he fills a large red sack with toys for the children of the world and then, carrying it on his back, climbs aboard his sleigh, where he deposits the gifts in a deep well behind his seat. He then flies through the air around the world, his sleigh pulled by eight reindeer who have the magical ability to fly. Their names have become legendary and are celebrated in literature and song: Dasher, Prancer, Vixen, Comet, Cupid, Donner, and Blitzen. In some stories, the names of the last two reindeer are rendered as Donder and Blixem. The names are derived from a poem written by Clement Moore in 1823 called A Visit from St. Nicholas, although the more popular name for this story is The Night Before Christmas. It is recited to children across the world, usually on Christmas Eve, as a way of preparing them for Santa's yearly visit. It lays forth much of what was mentioned above and certainly is one of the main sources for the myth of Santa Claus and what he does.

Sometimes a ninth reindeer is added, and his name is Rudolph, otherwise called Rudolph the Red-Nosed Reindeer. The story of Rudolph originated with the 1929 story by Robert L. May, Rudolph the Red-Nosed Reindeer. The legend of Rudolph skyrocketed, however, thanks to the song "Rudolph the Red-Nosed Reindeer" by cowboy, actor, and singer Gene Autrey. Rudolph's fame has been bolstered further over the years by countless cartoons, animations, and movies about the reindeer who supposedly is the head reindeer, one who has a red nose that blinks as he flies through the air when it's a foggy night. Rudolph, however, was not featured in The Night Before Christmas.

According to this story, Santa lands on the roofs of houses across the seven continents, slides down chimneys with his bag of toys and, after filling stockings hung on the mantlepiece, deposits presents under the family Christmas tree. Santa knows what presents to bring, of course, because children write him letters addressed to the North Pole in the months leading up to Christmas. In point of fact, the United States Post Office has a longstanding tradition of accepting these letters and sending them to a central location rather than merely throwing them away (at least in the short term). This is seen in the iconic black and white film Miracle on 34th Street, in which the existence of Santa is proven in court when the thousands of letters sent to Santa in New York are dumped in front of a judge. The court's ruling is that a man named Kris (Kris Kringle, that is) is indeed the true Santa. We'll discuss the movie in greater detail in a later chapter.

When it comes to the existence of Santa Claus, another claim to his true nature and reality appeared in the form of a Sun newspaper article in New York titled "Is There a Santa Claus?" The newspaper had previously received a letter from eight-year-old Virginia O'Hanlon asking the question paramount in the minds of many children as they grow older: Is Santa Claus real? The editorial stated that as long as people continued to exhibit the true spirit, love, and giving of the Christmas season, Santa would always be a reality in the lives of those who celebrated Christmas. Using today's terminology, the newspaper editorial went viral, and it was published in thousands of papers around the globe and is still done so today, this being yet another Christmas tradition that is part of the holiday season.

The visual image of Santa was also enhanced in 1863 when cartoonist Thomas Nast illustrated Santa visiting a Civil War encampment and distributing presents to Union soldiers. He is dressed in a fashion somewhat similar to that described above, and although this image helped to further popularize the image and legend of Santa, some of the toys were wooden carvings of Confederate President Jefferson Davis with a noose around his neck. It seems that jolly Saint Nick, at least in this rendition, had political sympathies that were not entirely in keeping with the love and generosity of the Christmas spirit. Nevertheless, the cartoon (and others by Nast) drew national and international attention and increased the legend and popularity of Santa Claus. You'll have noticed by now that the names Santa Claus and Saint Nick (or Saint Nicholas) have been used interchangeably, and this will be the subject of much discussion in subsequent chapters in which the origins and evolution of the concept of Santa are discussed.

Santa Claus, however, has not always been received favorably by everyone, both in the United States and Europe. As far back as Martin Luther and the Protestant Reformation, the idea of giving gifts at Christmastime was frowned upon since it supposedly detracted

Christians from focusing on the true meaning of Christmas, namely the birth of Christ. In later centuries and even in modern times, more conservative Christian denominations, especially evangelicals, have likewise criticized the commercialism of Christmas and the figure of Santa Claus. Pat Robertson, the evangelical preacher and CEO of the Christian Broadcasting Network (or CBN, which airs The 700 Club), has stated that Santa is a superstitious distraction for children, who attribute the supernatural abilities of God to a mythical being who, he believes, is practically worshipped by tens of millions of people. Robertson and many others have argued that the tradition of Santa Claus should be discontinued altogether since, according to Bible Belt theology, belief in Santa Claus is tantamount to heresy. These arguments against Saint Nick obviously have never gained traction as seen by depictions of Santa in hundreds of movies, television programs, books, cartoons, and (perhaps more than anything else), in advertising.

Likewise, the tradition of Santa Claus is discouraged and even banned in many oppressive political regimes, especially those that are communist since the image of Santa is inextricably linked to religion and the birth of Christ. In countries such as Russia and China, for example, the celebration of Christmas has been discouraged for many decades. In more modern times, Russia has eased sanctions on religious celebrations, and it is not uncommon to see depictions of Santa (or his cultural equivalent) during the holidays. China and North Korea, however, have always taken a much harder stance against the celebration of Christmas and the depiction of Santa, and many who choose to honor the birth of Christ in these countries face imprisonment (and in the past, even death).

In the face of so many detractors, it is nothing short of miraculous that the tradition of Santa Claus, call him whatever you will, has endured for over sixteen hundred years (and in pagan form for longer than that). Indeed, he has become a beloved, endearing figure who is hard to dislike. Santa's arrival on his sleigh at the end of the Macy's Thanksgiving Day Parade in New York City, officially opens the beginning of the holiday season in the U. S. In the weeks that follow, thousands of department store Santas may be seen in stores and malls across the United States, a custom that has also taken hold in Europe. Children are brought to sit on his lap and tell them what they want for Christmas. This, of course, is a masterful marketing tool since children know just what to ask for after browsing toy departments. Department store Santas, however, can be problematical. A common question among children is, that if Santa is one person who lives at the North Pole, why are there so many in cities across America, and why isn't he at his workshop preparing for his annual Christmas Eve ride. The answer by most thoughtful parents is that these are Santa's helpers, and given the dozens of traditions about the jolly old man and the longstanding position he has held in numerous cultures (not to mention the grip he has on the imaginations of both children and adults alike), the answer seems sufficient to quell any doubt in the minds of children who are already heavily invested in magic, toys, winter wonderlands, and Santa Claus.

Most children grow out of the belief of a literal Santa Claus by the age of seven or eight, if not younger, and yet the image of the man in the red suit is so pervasive in Western culture that one can safely say that the belief in Jolly Old Saint Nick never disappears completely. Perhaps, as was told to Virginia O'Hanlon, there is indeed a Santa Claus as long as people elect to keep alive his story and reenact the custom of putting toys under the Christmas tree—as long as they decide to emphasize the season as one of giving and kindness and love. And maybe there is a Santa in the minds of adults as well, or at least those who elect to keep alive a certain innocence of spirit and, as the Greeks put it, the willing suspension of belief in the art of storytelling. As numerous ministers over the decades have expressed, we denigrate the very supernatural Santa at our own peril in light of the fact that Christians believe in the supernatural virgin birth of Christ, who claimed to come from God, rise from the dead, and return to an everlasting invisible kingdom for eternity, where "all good children"—those who have not been naughty— are destined to go after death. Maybe that is why Santa is an ideal symbol of Christmas. He is a kind and loving man who gives of himself in ways that are not fully understood. In a very real sense, Santa Claus is linked to the birth of Christ despite what evangelicals may say to the contrary.

But there is an even more pressing question. Can it be possible that Santa is indeed real? Or put another way, was there ever a time when someone fitting Santa's description delivered presents at Christmastime? Is there a basis in the legend?

The answer is an unqualified "yes," and that is what we shall talk about next.

CHAPTER TWO
The Origins of Saint Nicholas

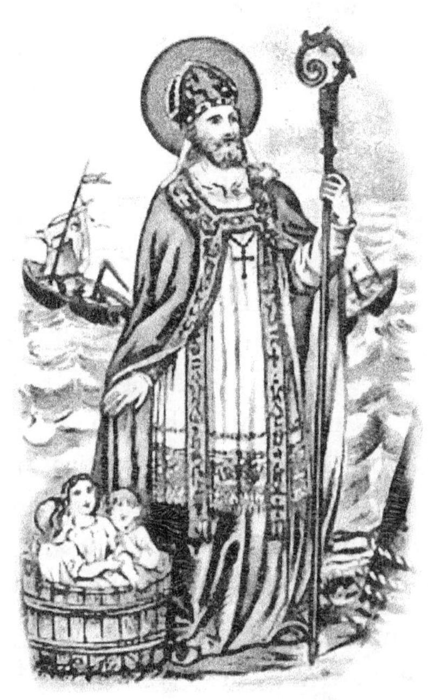

Bishop Nicholas of Myra lived from 270 A.D. to 343 A.D., and yet he is the figure upon which Santas from all countries are based. Yes, there was a real, historical Santa, and he is pictured here with his bishop's miter and crozier. Nicholas was later canonized by the Catholic Church, which is why he came to be called Saint Nicholas, a name that is synonymous with Santa in almost every land!

Many believe, and with good reason, that Bishop Nicholas of Myra was the real Santa Claus. Bishop Nicholas, now referred to in the Catholic Church as Saint Nicholas, lived in the town of Myra in Asia Minor (now modern-day Turkey) from 270 A.D. to 343 A.D. In the Catholic tradition, many miracles were attributed to this man, who became the patron saint of merchants, sailors, students, children, repentant thieves, and those who are unmarried. He has always been remembered, therefore, as someone who was kind and forgiving to many, and his habit of secretly giving gifts to people eventually gave birth the concept of Santa Claus. Hence, the evolution of Saint Nicholas, or more commonly just Saint Nick. The correlations between the bishop and Santa are unmistakable.

Another legend associated with Bishop Nicholas, and one that lends further credence to his being someone who gave gifts, especially to those in need, states that he allegedly saved three young women from a life of prostitution by dropping a sack of gold coins though the window of their home so that their father could pay for their dowries and thus make it possible for them to be married rather than force them into a life of selling their bodies to earn money for the family. The father, it is written, was once a wealthy merchant who lost his fortune after being attacked by Satan, his life thereafter falling into poverty and misfortune. The end of the story purports that the father caught Nicholas in the act of tossing the sacks of coins into his home and fell at the knees of his kindly benefactor. But Nicholas, it is said, ordered him to tell no one about his good deeds. In some versions of this tale, the sacks of gold coins are, in actuality, three gold balls of great value. Many scholars and historians have concluded that this may well be the origin of the custom of Santa Claus leaving apples, oranges, and other fruit in the stockings of children.

The secretiveness of Nicholas' action coincides with the modern-day tales that Santa Claus always visits homes at night and prefers that his gift-giving be performed under the cloak of darkness in order to preserve his humility and to increase the faith of those who find his presents the next morning, namely to believe in something that they can't see. This directly ties Saint Nicholas to the idea of believing in Christ and God, whose presence and kingdom cannot be accessed except through faith. It can be reliably argued that the tradition of Santa Claus and the true meaning of Christmas are aligned more closely than is commonly perceived and further argues against the evangelical notion that Santa Claus is nothing more than a pagan idea or, at best, a deception to children of the world.

It is also said that Nicholas raised the dead, cured the sick, and performed many miracles, such as calming a storm. These stories may be apocryphal, but they all contributed to the legend of a man who was able to operate on a supernatural level in support of charitable causes and service to others. The fact that he is often portrayed in art wearing red ecclesiastical robes and coats certainly does nothing to detract from the further alignment of the bishop with the figure of Santa Claus. It does not require much of leap of the imagination to see Santa's floppy red fur hat as evolving from the conical-shaped bishop's miter worn by Nicholas.

Bishop Nicholas therefore had a reputation for giving gifts, as well as food and clothing, to the poor and needy, this being part of his apostolic duties as a member of the Roman Catholic clergy. Other stories claim that he always deposited coins or other gifts, such as small toys or candy, in the shoes of children who left their footwear out on the night of December 5th. Saint Nicholas's feast day is December 6th, and therefore the idea of children receiving gifts the night before a holiday can also be traced directly to Bishop Nicholas whether one believes the stories to be literally true or not. The correspondence here is obvious: children hang their stockings on the mantle by the chimney the night before Christmas in the hopes that Saint Nick will leave them small gifts before depositing larger presents under the Christmas tree. In the long run, it makes little difference whether one envisions the receptacles to be shoes or stockings.

Saint Nicholas Day is celebrated on December 6th in much of the world. In some countries, it is simply one of many feasts and holidays that precede the main holiday of Christmas on December 25th. In some countries, however, December 6th gained more prominence and is as important (if not more so) as Christmas Day itself. In these countries, it is on December 5th and December 6th that the exchange of gifts (or a visit from Saint Nick) takes place, and the day is furthermore held in higher esteem because of the reputation of Saint Nicholas as described above. Although Saint Nicholas Day is not marked on most calendars in the United States, many countries choose to have great celebrations on this day, including large Christmas meals usually associated with Christmas Day. Some countries stage Christmas pageants on this day, as well gatherings to sing Christmas carols or reenactments of the Nativity. These traditions may be found to a greater or lesser extent in the following countries: the Netherlands, Luxembourg, Germany, France, Italy, and Portugal. Saint Nicholas Day is especially important in Eastern European and Slavic countries, many of which practice Christian Orthodox forms of Christianity, such as in Greece, Turkey, Russia, Slovakia, and several others. The fact that the celebration of the historical Saint Nicholas is so important to millions of people around the world is further testament to the conflation of Saint Nick with Santa Claus.

But there are many other figures who represent intermediate steps between Bishop Nicholas and the modern-day Santa we see in movies and films in the twenty-first century. The first of these is known as Sinterklaas, and that is who we will examine next.

CHAPTER THREE
Sinterklaas

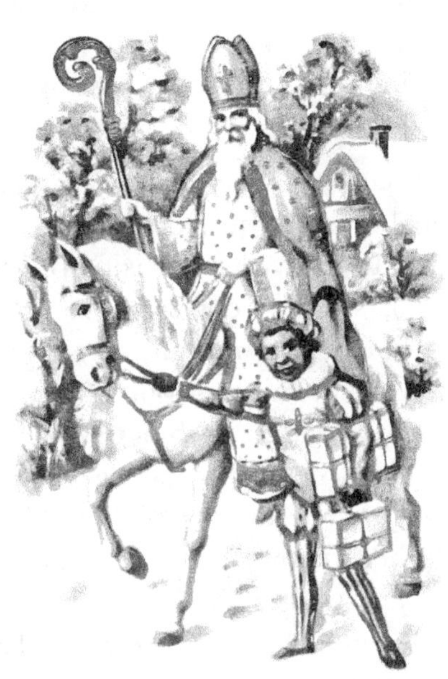

Sinterklaas is the Dutch name for Santa Claus, and he is seen accompanied by his helper named Black Pete. Sinterklaas may look like Bishop Nicholas here, but he was the Santa who evolved into the modern Saint Nick when he was exported to the New World and written about by American poets and authors.

Santa Claus as we know him today in Western culture and across much of the world stemmed from Dutch beliefs about Saint Nicholas, who in the Dutch language is called Sinterklaas. Dutch explorers settled in the New World in a region they termed New Amsterdam, Amsterdam being the capital of the Netherlands. New Amsterdam was a rather large region in North America in territories now drawn into the states of New York, New Jersey, and Connecticut. It was established in 1624 by the Dutch West India Trading Company. The settlers brought with them the legend of Sinterklaas, or Saint Nicholas, who became part of Christmas celebrations in the New World. This was a time when the evolution of Bishop Nicholas of Myra as Santa Claus accelerated and eventually became the jolly figure we know today as Santa.

The representation of Saint Nicholas had by this time already undergone transformation as Saint Nicholas was now painted as a portly figure dressed in a red robe (sometimes a red chasuble, the outer garment worn by priests saying mass), and a tall red miter. He was depicted as having long, curly, white hair and a long white beard. He also carried with him a red book that supposedly had the names of children who had behaved or misbehaved during the previous year.

According to Dutch tradition, Sinterklaas was accompanied by a figure known as Zwarte Piet, or Black Pete, a character who is one of the earliest personages to be called "Santa's helper." We'll talk about Santa's helpers in later chapters.

Before coming to the New World, the Dutch held Sinterklaasfest during the Middle Ages, a feast that was both holy and vulgar. It was at this time that the tradition of putting coins and candy in the shoes of children became more widespread, but the feast was also marked by a great deal of partying and public drunkenness. That having been said, students at religious schools would take turns dressing up as Bishop Nicholas and reenact events from the saint's life.

This brings us again to the nineteenth century, when Jan Schenkman wrote Saint Nicholas and His Servant in 1850. (In this story, Santa rides a horse.) But this is long after Clement Moore wrote A Visit from St. Nicholas (The Night Before Christmas), so how could Moore have capitalized on a Dutch story written decades after him. The answer lies in scholarship connecting these two different yet similar accounts of Saint Nicholas's trip on Christmas Eve. As early as 1812, Washington Irving, considered one of the great writers in early American literature, wrote a Christmas story that drew heavily on the Dutch traditions of Sinterklaas. Nine years later, this story was embellished further by author William Gilley. It is believed that Clement Moore, writing in 1823, synthesized existing Dutch material and codified it for generations to come in The Night Before Christmas, altering some elements to bring it in line to who we know as Santa today. The horse was obviously changed to reindeer, the sleigh was added, and Santa's helpers became the harmless and helpful elves who lived at the North Pole and did not accompany Saint Nick on his yearly round to deliver gifts. The notion that naughty children would receive a lump of coal in their stockings instead of presents is not present in Moore's poem, and yet it is a piece of folklore that is very much an outgrowth of the earlier traditions in which figures such as Black Pete would punish naughty children or leave them less than desirable gifts in place of those that had been requested.

In modern times, a festival in the Netherlands is held yearly to celebrate the arrival by steamboat of Sinterklaas from Spain. He arrives in Antwerp, although in cities that are landlocked, he may arrive by train or motor vehicles. The reason that Sinterklaas arrives from Spain is because relics thought to be those of Saint Nicholas were discovered in the Italian city of Bari, a city that was later incorporated into the Spanish kingdom of Naples. As incredible as it may seem, however, the other reasons why Sinterklaas is believed to hail from Spain rather than the

North Pole is because Saint Nick was thought, as previously mentioned, to dispense oranges, pomegranates, and other fruit on Christmas Eve, these fruits being indigenous to Spain. The other reason is that Black Pete was a Moor, and Moors are a segment of Spain's population that are of African-American descent because of racial intermarriage.

Regardless of how or where Sinterklaas arrives in the Netherlands, parades are held after he steps from the steamboat, train, or other vehicle (even a horse or carriage), and he and Black Pete ride in the parade, throwing candy and small trinkets to the crowd. It is a major holiday, and the arrival and parade are broadcast on national television. While Sinterklaas still looks more like the red-robed Saint Nicholas than the American Santa Claus, the resemblance is now close enough so that the two figures have almost merged in the cultural consciousness of those countries, previously named, that honor Saint Nicholas (or Sinterklaas, depending on the language spoken in the country that celebrates Saint Nicholas Day). Indeed, the figures have merged so much over the years that, in the movie Miracle on 34th Street, a young girl is overheard talking to in the department store as she waits in line to speak with Santa, and she converses in Dutch with a man called Sinterklaas.

In those countries that celebrate Saint Nicholas Day, children and parents leave out hay or carrots for the horse of Sinterklaas, and they also leave coffee or beer for Sinterklaas and Black Pete. Leaving bits of food for Saint Nick became the custom of putting out milk and cookies for Santa on Christmas Eve. On December 6th, children get up early and check for presents just as other children check for presents on Christmas morning. Older children, those who have grown beyond the age at which they can accept a magical figure such as Saint Nick, exchange gifts with each other, parents, or other adults, often in a custom that is practiced in many countries, namely that of the Secret Santa.

It should be obvious by now that there is a direct line connecting Bishop Nicholas of Myra to Saint Nicholas, which then evolved over many years and in many cultures into Sinterklaas, a man who is obviously the precursor to the Santa Claus known by most of the Western World. It should be noted that in many countries, Santa Claus (or Saint Nick) is not mutually exclusive to the existence of Sinterklaas. In European countries (France, Italy, Spain, and Eastern European or Slavic countries), Saint

Nicholas Day is simply one more day in the Christmas season that begins with Advent (usually beginning in late November or early December). Saint Nicholas is honored (and even venerated, together with the relics of his bones) as a goodly Christian man who practiced the Christmas spirit centuries ago. It is yet another religious connection between the figure of Santa and the birth of Christ.

The fact that so many countries and cultures throughout the world regard Santa, Saint Nicholas, Saint Nick, and Sinterklaas as the primary gift-giver on either December 5th or December 24th is a testament to the fact that Santa, whatever name is ascribed to him, is a worldwide phenomenon. It can also be seen that the evolution of the character, beginning with Bishop Nicholas of Myra, encompassed dozens (and ultimately hundreds) of different cultures, eventually commingling with local customs and producing Christmas traditions regarding Santa and the way gifts are received. Many of these will be discussed in greater detail in later chapters since they relate directly to the collection of Santa Clauses I have in Great Bend. The above is really only the tip of the iceberg because the way Santa is dressed and depicted in drawings, paintings, and statues around the world is indeed diverse. Almost all costumes are variations on the traditional theme, although the color of his garb as well as the appearance of his shoes, boots, hats, coats, and belts may differ depending on how the tradition of Santa was assimilated by any given culture, where it may or may not have merged with existing or older traditions of a figure, usually pagan, who delivers presents at Christmastime.

It is important to note that some countries do not honor the tradition of Santa at all, and even in those that do, other figures replace the character of Santa as someone who visits yearly on or around Christmas. Some of these are Befana, Belsnickel, Krampus, the Yule Goat, and dozens of others, and these will receive treatment in later chapters as well. What is important to note at this point is that the celebration of Christmas on December 25th resulted from a rather arbitrary decision made in the third century by Roman Emperor Constantine, who declared upon his ascendancy to the throne that the birth of Christ would be celebrated on December 25th because this date, according to the Julian calendar used by Rome, was the date of the winter solstice, or the shortest day of the year. The real solstice occurs on December 21st according to the modern-day Gregorian calendar, but the salient point is that Constantine wanted to replace pagan festivals, usually marked by heavy drinking and orgiastic behavior, with those commensurate with the religion he'd adopted for the Roman Empire. Religion in any country has the potential to be a stabilizing influence. To help eradicate Roman paganism by degrees, the winter solstice was therefore Christianized and replaced with celebrations far tamer and certainly more religious in spirit. Scholars are quite settled in the belief that Christ was actually born sometime in April in the year 4 B.C., but this fact has been lost over the centuries as Christmas became a worldwide celebration during winter.

Nevertheless, many pagan figures from ancient times have survived even in the present day. Some of these pagan and alternate figures were friendly and rewarding, while others were sinister or downright evil. Some even presided over the aforementioned orgies and pagan rites, which included human sacrifice.

And yet it has been Saint Nick, Santa Claus, and his other iterations that have survived into the twenty-first century and are regarded as some of the most notable figures of any Christmas celebration regardless of where in the world the holiday is celebrated. But Sinterklaas is only one of many precursors to the contemporary American Santa Claus. The next is uniquely British is sentiment.

CHAPTER FOUR
Father Christmas

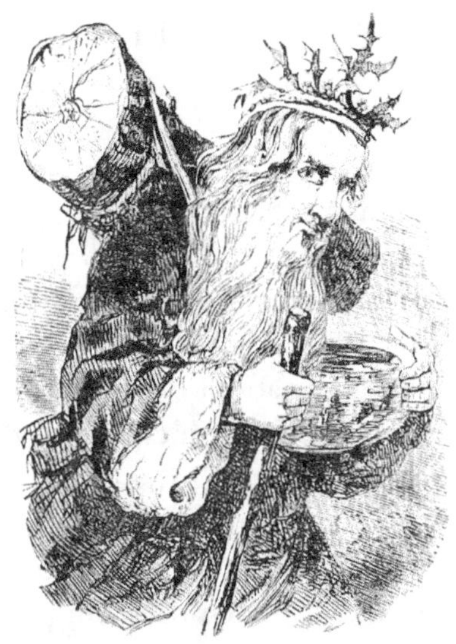

England has always called Santa Claus Father Christmas because ... well, the British have a different idiom from American English. In the UK, Father Christmas has been the personification of the holiday season since Celtic times. He is seen here carrying a Yule Log and almost looks like the Santa we know today!

There is a separate tradition that also leads to the persona of Santa Claus, one that takes a different historical trajectory than that discussed in the previous chapter but one that eventually merges with it in the nineteenth and twentieth centuries. English tradition for centuries has embraced a figure who is called Father Christmas, who originally was a male figure who was considered to be the personification of the Christmas season, someone who represented the entire meaning of Christmastime, from the birth of Christ to gift-giving, decorations, and holiday celebrations and merry-making.

Some historians believe that Father Christmas has his roots in early Celtic traditions in Britain, where Christianity began to take root between the second and fourth centuries because of missionaries from Europe as well as the Roman conquest of the island by Julius Caesar around 60 A.D. Although Caesar brought Roman culture and its pagan mythology to the British Isles, later travelers from the provinces of the Roman Empire imported Christian rituals that were slowly gaining traction in Europe, albeit under persecution until Emperor Constantine, as seen in the previous chapter, finally declared Christianity to be the official state religion.

Between the fourth and eleventh centuries, Britain experienced several waves of Viking invasions, mostly from Scandinavia but also from the Germanic tribes of Northern Europe. These tribes were the Angles, Saxons, and Jutes, and the first two tribes represent the origin of the word "Anglo-Saxon" as a term to refer to the heritage of the English. More to the point, the Vikings exported Norse pagan mythology to Great Britain, but as the centuries passed, missionaries would return with these invaders to Scandinavia, which began to undergo its own stages of Christianization. What happened was a cross-pollination of cultures, in which pagan ideas infiltrated early Christian beliefs, while Christianity gradually affected and transformed Norse mythology, which has as many gods and goddesses and the mythologies of Greece and Rome. Christian celebrations in what is now England, therefore, bore elements that were essentially Christian in nature but still honored some of the older Norse deities and customs. Many of these customs revolved around the celebration of the winter solstice on or about December 21st and also involved orgies and heavy-duty partying that included nudity and drunkenness. In other words, Christmas in England was a time for celebrating the birth of Christ, but that celebration was highly diversified and contained elements of dozens of different cultures in Scandinavia and Europe as well as numerous Celtic traditions, much of them pagan in nature, that had exited from before the birth of Christ.

Father Christmas, therefore, derived from the folkloric traditions in England that came from many different areas of Europe. Until Victorian times, Father Christmas represented the tradition of feasting and merry-making in general, most of it fit only for adults and having little to do with God, innocence, or children. Christ was always in the background as the backbone of the celebration, but Christmas as a blessed season only took hold gradually. Father Christmas originally had no direct role in giving presents to children, sliding down chimneys, carrying a sack of toys, or using a sleigh and reindeer. This particular personification was imagined to dress in robes, sometimes red, and carry sacks of beverages (usually alcohol), and he wore a crown made from holly branches and carried a staff. Strapped to his back was a Yule log that was to be burnt in fireplaces at times of feasting. While this figure has as much to do with pagan traditions as it does with Christian ones, it is obvious that this representation does indeed bear similarities to the figure that would later be known as Santa Claus.

The exact date on which the character of Father Christmas emerged is not known with any certitude, although it is believed that he may have existed in various forms and garb as early as the aforementioned Celtic times and, as stated, may have even originated from certain figures common in Norse mythology. In fact, many believe that at least some of England's Christmas traditions were direct offshoots of Scandinavian custom, and much has been written about "the pagan roots of Christmas." The Norse god Odin, the chief deity in the Norse pantheon, was believed to be an old man with a long white beard who wore a heavy fur cloak and rode across the sky on an eight-legged horse to deliver presents during mid-winter festivals. This certainly parallels the more obvious traits of the modern Santa Claus.

But the Norse traditions go deeper than this when we consider how they might have been conflated with Christmas traditions that included elves, Christmas trees, holly, mistletoe, wreaths, Yule logs, the twelve days of Christmas, and the Christmas ham. Today, these various objects are all intimately associated with Christmastime and have been incorporated into world cultures in a distinctly Christian way. For the Norse populations, their midwinter celebration was called Yule, and they feasted on ham and other fare while burning Yule logs in the hearths of both homes, lodges, and mead halls (such as those described in the epic English poem of Scandinavian and Celtic origin titled Beowulf). The feasting, presided over by a figure such as Odin and later called Father Christmas, entailed imbibing large quantities of mead, a beverage that was similar to homemade mulled wine or, in some cases, beer. Mistletoe was very popular, as it was hung above doorways or from rafters, and those men and women who passed beneath it were expected to kiss each other—and actually do a whole lot more—so even in this well-known tradition we can see that its origins were rooted in pagan feasting and rather rampant sexual activity. As for elves, in Norse mythology they were thought to be tall creatures with pointed ears, beings who possessed magical powers. Later, they were described in tales passed down by word of mouth as small gnome-like creatures who wore pointed red caps and helped with the duties associated with the Yule festivities. We'll have a lot more to say about elves later.

It is easy to see how these creatures came to be regarded as Santa's helpers. As for the ham, Vikings killed wild boars and pigs in order to sacrifice them to the Norse god Freyr in hopes that the coming year would be blessed with fertile crops. While this custom has more in common with Easter, in which the pascal lamb is sacrificed to please God the Father in Christianity, the idea of sacrifice and the coming of a savior to bring better and more blessed times is nevertheless present in the Norse sacrificial tradition. The celebration began on the winter solstice, a time to feast and appease the gods in hopes of a fruitful spring, and lasted for twelve days, this being a precursor to what we now call The Twelve Days of Christmas. Finally, Scandinavians loved to decorate the many kinds of fir trees so prevalent in their forests and on their hillsides. They decorated the branches with small carvings that were likenesses of pagan deities, and this bears a strong resemblance to the custom of hanging Christian-themed ornaments on modern Christmas trees.

By the fifteenth century, the god Odin had begun to resemble Father Christmas during the midwinter celebration of Yule in Scandinavia, parts of Europe, and in England. Carols emerged about this time, and their theme was that people should be merry and jolly as they feasted during the twelve days of Christmas. At times, various town leaders were crowned as "Kings of Christmas," and in such cases these figures bore a strong resemblance to Father Christmas. The personification of the season was beginning to acquire a more and recognizable human form that would lead to Santa.

In later centuries, these midwinter celebrations would slowly lose their pagan connotations as conventional Christianity, now taking much stronger hold in Europe, adopted and transformed the traditions described above, and this included the character of Father Christmas. Somewhere between the eleventh and sixteenth centuries, for example, the word Yule was replaced in England with the term Christmas, a word that literally meant the "mass of Christ." That having been said, the word "Yule" has remained part of the vernacular of Christmastime and is often synonymous with the word Christmas itself. This didn't mean that feasting and heavy drinking were not part of the season, however.

During the classic periods of English history, such as the rule of the Tudors (think in terms of the very opulent and lusty King Henry VIII and his eight wives), Father Christmas took on many different titles and was seen dressed in various attire, although most resembled the earlier description of him given in this chapter. Some of these personifications of the season were known as Prince Christmas, The Christmas Lord, and even the Lord of Misrule, the latter title still hearkening back to a more unruly and pagan aspect of the Christmas celebration. Still, as more and more time passed, the figure of Father Christmas, looking more and more like Santa (or Saint Nick or Sinterklaas) would show up at festive gatherings or feasting halls where large Christmas dinners were held, these now starting to serve such dishes as roast turkey, goose, or ham. Often, Father Christmas would preside over these dinners, and it was common for him and the many guests to drink wassail punch, usually a strong beverage that combined various fruit juices with alcohol. Even later, a custom called wassailing would emerge in England, a tradition that called for people to go from door to door and sing carols in exchange for small gifts such as candies, wassail, and small baked (and heavily-spiced) breads called soal cakes. The word "soal" was an alternate spelling of the word "soul." This is one of many English holiday customs, but it should be remembered that it was Father Christmas who was the face of the season and represented in broad strokes all of the festivities of the holiday.

As noted earlier, the Protestant Reformation took a dim view of the more mirthful and extroverted celebrations of Christmas, regarding them as lewd, worldly, and unholy. Since Father Christmas was even more permissive in his feasting than the figures of Saint Nicholas or Sinterklaas, he was greatly frowned upon by all of those who had adopted Martin Luther's very stringent and puritanical approach to honoring of the Christmas season. Indeed, Puritans in England and later in the thirteen colonies in America regarded Christmas Day as a time for sober reflection on the salvation afforded by Christ, who had come into the world to save men from their sins, and that included any kind of heavy drinking (or drinking at all) in addition to the general feasting common at this time of year. To counter the puritanical attitude towards a season that had always been marked by a spirit of jolliness and merrymaking, even when tame, some politicians, playwrights, and authors (such as Ben Jonson) would dress up in red clothes, white ruffled collars, long white stockings, and long white beards. These personages were called Lord Christmas or Sir Christmas, but in time they were simply referred to as Father Christmas, and their attire, while varied depending on the play or pageant in which they were featured, did bear a striking similarity to the Norse version of Father Christmas.

When the English monarchy was suspended in the 1600s by head of state Oliver Cromwell, Christmas was banned, as were depictions of any kind of figure personifying the season, and that included Father Christmas, Saint Nicholas, and Sinterklaas—but mainly Father Christmas since his character was dominant over the others in English culture, while other parts of Europe continued with celebrations featuring Saint Nicholas and Sinterklaas. With the revival of the monarchy in 1660 and the return of King Charles II to the throne, the Christmas celebration was reinstated. Christmas feasts were again common throughout the population, both upper and lower classes, and it was common to have a traditional Christmas dinner that included roast (the English are nicknamed "Beefeaters"), turkey, goose, ham, puddings, wassail, cranberries, and many different kinds of dessert. But the Puritans had managed to leave an indelible mark on the holiday, and by the seventeenth century, the celebration of Christmas, while still a time for feasting, was more in keeping with "proper English behavior" and resembled the Christmas that would be honored over the next three centuries. It is most interesting to note that Father Christmas made his return, but he was now pictured as a man who was closer to Saint Nicholas, and in addition to his long white hair and beard, he wore a heavy red cloak and a hat that was now neither a religious miter or a crown of holly branches. It was now a red fur cap with white piping at its bottom. The similarity to Santa Claus was now growing stronger with each passing decade, and new illustrations were made of the man who was now a gift-giver to children and who honored the Christian origins of the season and the true meaning of Christmas, meaning the birth of Christ. If nothing else, the Puritans had managed to shape Christmas into a decidedly more religious holiday even though feasting would never entirely drop out of the picture.

Father Christmas enjoyed an especially powerful revival during the Victorian period, certainly not known for its wild parties, and by 1843, when Charles Dickens published his novella A Christmas Carol, the celebration of Christmas, as seen in the very popular story that has been made into dozens of motion pictures, was firmly entrenched in the English mindset—and so was Father Christmas. As time wore on, the United States, having won its independence from England, established diplomatic ties with Great Britain, and the figure of Santa Claus, now strongly embedded in the American psyche thanks to Saint Nicholas having emerged as the recognizable gift-giver dressed in red and riding a sleigh pulled by reindeer, became more and more conflated with Father Christmas. But British idiom is often quite different than American English, and to this day the British usually refer to Santa Claus as Father Christmas even though the figure of Santa Claus is well-known and sometimes substituted for the older moniker of Father Christmas.

CHAPTER FIVE
Samichlaus

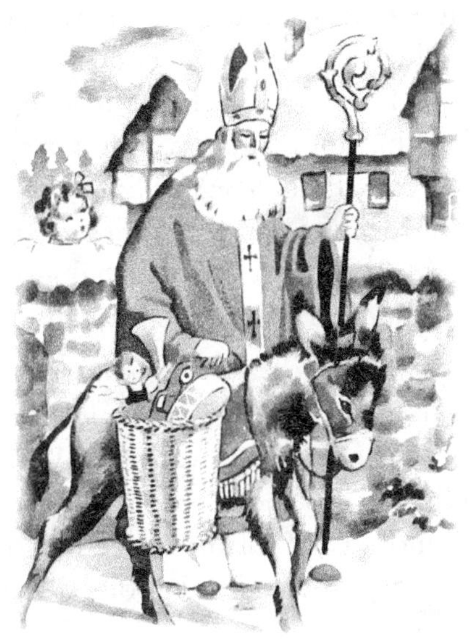

Samichlaus is the Polish equivalent of Santa Claus and looks similar to Sinterklaas. He's a gift-giver like all the others although he moves a bit more slowly on the donkey that symbolizes the one that Mary rode to Bethlehem. Notice he's still wearing a bishop's miter just like Saint Nicholas. The tradition of Santa spread quickly throughout Eastern Europe, and Samichlaus was one of the earlier versions of Saint Nick.

We have seen that Bishop Nicholas of Myra gave birth to Saint Nicholas, Saint Nick, Sinterklaas, and Father Christmas. These figures are all variations on a theme and derive from the Christian tradition of celebrating Christ's birth by the giving of gifts to reflect what Christians regard as God's ultimate gift to the world, that being Jesus Christ. The giving of gifts also derives from the gifts given to the Christ Child by The Three Wise Men, or The Magi, as they were known, and we shall discuss these kings in greater detail later. Ultimately, however, the tradition of giving and receiving presents stems from Bishop Nicholas, although many have hypothesized that the bishop's philanthropic attitude towards children and the poor reflects this same core principle that the birth of Christ in Bethlehem is the first and most important gift of the Christmas season, one to be emulated by giving, in turn, gifts to others. While Bishop Nicholas did indeed give toys and treats to children, much of his distributed bounty was food, clothing, and other necessities that were given to the poor and needy, a fact that tallies with basic Christian concerns for the downtrodden and less fortunate.

This dual role of gift-giving—toys versus food and necessities—is still present in Christmas traditions in the twenty-first century. The emphasis on Santa Claus delivering toys and goodies to children remains as steadfast as ever, although one need only tune into local or national newscasts at Christmastime to see that tens of thousands of people across the world devote their time to distributing cold-weather clothing to the needy and volunteering to serve holiday meals at homeless shelters as well as manning free medical clinics for those who cannot afford healthcare. It's quite extraordinary, when one stops and thinks about it, that both of these traditions have survived so long, all derivative of the concept of a kindly man who loves unconditionally and gives good things to people without being asked. It's not surprising that more than a few parents, when confronted by their older children on whether or not Santa Claus is real, have replied by saying that, in a technical and historical sense, the answer is an unqualified yes. Although he may not have lived at the North Pole or driven a sleigh pulled by reindeer, Bishop Nicholas fits the archetype of Santa Claus with surprising accuracy.

But the various names, images, characteristics, and behaviors in terms of gift-giving extends far beyond the main characters we have already seen. While the evolution of Bishop Nicholas to the modern-day Santa Claus is fairly direct, the cultures of hundreds of countries across the globe have appropriated the persona of Saint Nick and molded it to fit their particular beliefs, folklore, seasonal traditions, and religious denominations. In many cases, the variations on the man known as Santa or Saint Nick are slight. He's still the man who dresses in warm red clothes and flies around the world on Christmas Eve even if cultural differences tweak his overall image somewhat. In other cases, the variations are more pronounced and resemble the Western version of Santa to a lesser degree. In yet other instances, the variations are quite pronounced and are the result of the commingling of pagan traditions (usually associated with the winter solstice) that date back thousands of years. Because Christianity and its attendant celebration of the birth of Christ, spread though Eastern and Western Europe unevenly and according to different timeframes, it's not at all surprising that the Christmas gift-giver can take so many different forms. As seen in the last chapter, the most obvious example is how Christianity and Santa Claus were intertwined with Celtic and Norse pagan traditions by the time the new religion had started to infiltrate the British Isles by the fourth century A.D. Nevertheless, Santa still evolved into a jolly, kindhearted man in Great Britain and in most of Western Europe, in which there was more trade and communication among countries such as Spain, Portugal, France, Italy, and Germany (not that these did not have their own takes on Santa Claus, as we shall see shortly). Eastern Europe, however, was a different matter, and so were most other countries around the world, where the folklore surrounding Santa (and Christmas traditions in general) found numerous expressions based on existing culture and customs.

Poland is a prime example. Santa is called Samichlaus, and because Poles identify most strongly with the original Santa, namely Bishop Nicholas of Myra, Samichlaus is portrayed as a bearded man dressed in canonical vestments and a miter, this religious garb looking very much the same as that worn by bishops in modern times. The miter is a tall cone-shaped hat that represents the tongues of fire that descended on the heads of the apostles on Pentecost, the fire representing the presence of the Holy Spirit. Poland is very Catholic, with the Eastern Orthodox religion representing the second-largest population of Christians in the country, and therefore the resemblance of their Santa to Bishop Nicholas is not surprising.

Samichlaus, however, is definitely the main bringer of presents at Christmastime. He delivers presents on Christmas Eve (since the New Year began on December 24th in the Middle Ages), but he doesn't drive a sleigh or fly through the air. Rather, he rides on a donkey plodding through the heavy winter snow, having left his humble cottage in northern Poland to deliver presents to eagerly-awaiting boys and girls. Some believe that Samichlaus rides a donkey merely as a sign of religious humility, while others go a step further and equate Samichlaus's journey with the journey that Mary and Joseph made to Bethlehem, where Mary should "deliver" the baby Jesus in a manger. As it stated in scripture and portrayed on Christmas cards, Mary rode a donkey. The parallels are almost too many to gloss over and are yet other signs of how closely Polish Christians wish Samichlaus to be identified with gospels narratives that describe the Nativity of Christ. This portrayal may lack the flare and magical powers associated with the airborne Santa known in the West, but it is nevertheless a charming variation on the figure of Santa. In the eyes of Poles, it is a portrayal that represents the best aspects of both Eastern and Western traditions.

An interesting postscript to Samichlaus is that he first arrives in a parade on December 6th, which is the Feast of Saint Nicholas, but this is seen by most countrymen as a dry run for the real event on Christmas

Eve. If children meet Samichlaus on December 6th, they may receive a present in exchange for reciting a poem or singing a song. Otherwise, Polish children (as is the custom in large areas of Europe) clean their shoes and leave them by the door of their homes on Christmas Eve in the hopes of receiving their presents. Children in America and other countries in the Western Hemisphere take a much bolder approach into the run-up to Christmas morning. They hang stockings on the mantel by the fireplace instead of placing shoes by the door, and they hope that Santa, after sliding down the chimney, will reward them by leaving the "really big stuff" under the Christmas tree. The stockings are for small treats, but the similarity between Eastern and Western cultural traditions is obvious. Repositories, so to speak, are left on Christmas Eve in the hope that they will be filled when the very special yearly guest arrives.

In some parts of Poland, as well as other areas of Eastern Europe, the bringer of toys and treats bears almost no resemblance to the kind of Santa Claus we've been discussing. The most notable exception to the tradition of Saint Nick in Poland is called Starman, a kindly figure who knocks on the door on Christmas Eve and then leaves after depositing a sack of goodies for children in the household. The sack of toys and their delivery date are the only real similarities between Starman and Santa. The tradition of Starman probably evolved from the eighteenth and nineteenth century tradition of carolers going from door to door, with one of the carolers carrying a staff with a star fixed to its top. Over time, the man carrying the staff was, for obvious reasons, called the "star man," now known as Starman. As time wore on, Starman, because of his name, was thought to be an otherworldly being who literally lived somewhere in the heavens and could fly down to Earth. These latter traits of the character echo the idea of a Santa, who can fly in a sleigh and lives at the North Pole which, while not otherworldly, is still a hiding place that no one can quite locate.

Even in this variation of a gift-giver, however, there are distant echoes of Saint Nicholas since bishops, when dressed in their ceremonial robes and performing various religious ceremonies, carry a staff, called a crozier. The staff represents a shepherd's crook because Christ proclaimed himself as the Good Shepherd, with Christian bishops supposedly taking his place as Christ's successors on earth. The top of the staff has always been curled (for easy handling in ancient times), and a bishop's crozier was stylized and made to resemble the crosier fern, which curls over many times in ornamental scrolls. With such ornamental work replacing a simple crook, the top of the staff came to be adorned with many Christian emblems, such as a cross, fish, globe (the Earth), or other ornamental carvings that had some relationship to Christian symbolism. It was only a matter of time before a star was set atop the staff given that The Three Wise Men followed the Christmas Star to Bethlehem. In a real sense, Starman leads us right back to Bishop Nicholas.

Since there is no real artistic representation of Starman other than as a shepherd or caroler, Starman in modern times dresses like the Santa Claus everyone is familiar with and often walks the streets, rides a float, or drives a car. The permutations are endless and reiterate our theme: folklore is liable to alter the history and depiction of Saint Nick in any number of ways so as to keep local customs alive while simultaneously adopting the larger legend known as Santa Claus.

A variation of Starman is The Little Angel, who is a female angel (often depicted as an innocent little girl). She descends from her heavenly home, the precise location of which is unknown, during the Christmas season in order to deliver presents just as Starman does. The association between the two figures is probably a result of the commonality of their heavenly homes somewhere in the sky. Angels have always been regarded as beings who live "up there," meaning heaven, which for thousands of years has been thought to be above the Earth, while hell and punishment are considered to be somewhere "down there," meaning below the Earth.

The ancient tradition of The Little Angel probably developed into a Santa substitute in modern times, one associated with gift-giving, because of the Christmas narratives in the biblical gospels of Saint Matthew and Saint Luke. In these documents, an angel appeared to shepherds tending their flocks (one assumes with staffs, or shepherd's crooks). More specifically, the angel appeared in the heavens—the sky—to announce the birth of the savior in the nearby town of Bethlehem. The angel announced "peace on Earth and to men of goodwill." But what else was in the sky on that night according to scripture? Why, the Christmas Star, of course, the very one that led The Wise Men to the stable where the new king of the world was to be born. As everyone knows, they arrived not only to pay homage to the Infant Jesus but to give him gifts.

It is easy to see, when looking through the lenses of the gospel accounts of Christ's birth, the confluence of the major aspects of the Christian traditions that coincide so closely with Santa Claus, Starman, and The Little Angel: a star, shepherds and their staffs (or bishop's crooks), travel through the sky, gift-giving, and the general kindness demonstrated by Santa towards people of the world.

Perhaps the figure of Samichlaus demonstrates more than any other Christmas personage discussed thus far how customs can evolve from existing traditions to suit the culture and folklore in a given country. Furthermore, Samichlaus and his counterparts—Starman and The Little Angel—clearly illustrate how Christianity has directly influenced various Santa figures to fit its ideology and doctrine. We shall see this commingling of folklore and the Christianization of Santa on an even larger scale in our next Santa, named Grandfather Frost.

CHAPTER SIX
Grandfather Frost

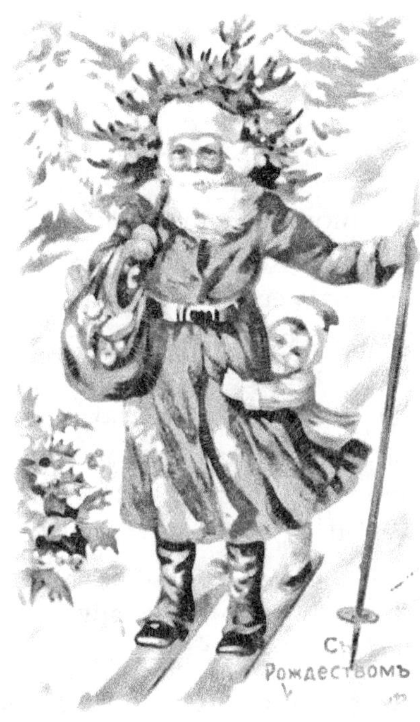

Grandfather Frost, or Ded Moroz, is the name for Santa in Russia. He evolved from a pagan snow wizard named Morozko, whose body was nothing more than wind and clouds, but he still had a long white beard. Over time, that beard was attached to Saint Nicholas rather than a snow wizard. He is pictured here with his helper, a snow maiden named Snegurochka. Who says Santa can't ski!

The name pretty much says it all. Grandfather Frost is the name given to Santa in Russia and many Slavic countries in Eastern Europe. Santa is often considered to be an older yet vigorous man, avuncular in every way. He is the wise old grandfather beloved in so many families, only Santa's family consists of the entire world. He is a man who likes to put his grandchildren on his knee, tell them stories, or listen to what they have been doing lately. This is certainly the image of Santa in thousands of department stores, where Santa listens carefully as young children recite what toys they want for Christmas. It is a picture both endearing and enduring and reflects the kindness and acceptance that we saw in the other Santas as well as in Starman and The Little Angel.

The word "frost" also speaks for itself. Frost occurs most often in the winter months around the time of the winter solstice. Frost also connotes wintertime scenes like those portrayed on Christmas cards and in Christmas movies. Santa drives a sleigh specifically because its runners can handle the thick snow and frost of wintertime. Frost and snow also create icicles that hang from the eaves of homes that Santa will visit, and hence we have the traditional icicle ornaments and tinsel that adorn Christmas trees around the world. In this respect, the terms Santa Claus and Grandfather Frost are almost synonymous—two expressions of the same figure.

That Grandfather Frost is a man who looks very much like Santa—sometimes exactly like him—in Russia and other Slavic countries in the twentieth and twenty-first centuries is therefore not surprising. The origins of Grandfather Frost, however, are not evenly remotely connected to any concept, modern or Christian, of Santa Claus. As we shall see, the figure of Grandfather Frost, as was the case with Samichlaus splitting into Starman and The Little Angel, assumed more than one form over the centuries.

According to Slavic legends dating back more than a thousand years, Grandfather Frost (called Ded Moroz—sometimes Dred Moroz) in most Eastern European languages) was a snow demon who could forge chains of bondage out of water and snow. He would often kidnap small children and return them to their parents in exchange for whatever gifts he demanded. This Wizard of Winter, as he was sometimes known, was allegedly the offspring of Veles and Mara, the pagan gods of spring. Going back two thousand years, his name was Morozko, and he could freeze people and other elements of the landscape—trees, lakes, rivers, animals, and mountains—simply by his stare. He was an arbitrary godlike figure who also dabbled in politics when he chose to freeze advancing armies and soldiers.

As the centuries wore on, the Russian Orthodox Church (similar to the Catholic Church in almost all ways except that it doesn't acknowledge the authority and infallibility of the pope in Rome) decided that it needed to tame this rather monstrous mythological creature who was known to appear and perform his mischief in late December. He was too much at odds with the image of the meek and mild Christ Child, who would, according to the Bible, grow into a man with power to heal sickness and perform miracles. The two supernatural figures couldn't have been more at odds with each other, so the Russian church decided to Christianize Morozko by giving him most (but not all) of the attributes of Saint Nicholas and Father Christmas. Instead of kidnapping, scaring, and torturing children, he would bring them presents assuming they had engaged in polite and appropriate behavior during the rest of the year.

When it came to appearances, Grandfather Frost wore many different outfits. He was most frequently portrayed as wearing bishop's robes—many layers of them—or wearing a cope, which is a wide Christian vestment that wraps around the body like a cape, although this one was very thick and lined with fur to protect against the harsh weather of winter. Sometimes he wore a bishop's miter, while other times he wore a crown, horns (obviously a throwback to his earlier demonic incarnations), furry cap, or some combination of the above, such as a small, furry, conical cap with horns arching over its top and meeting in the middle. In some respects, he resembled a Norse god attired in warm, furry animal skins and horns. Still, his mission was to bring presents to children, and no meanness was to be found in Grandfather Frost, or Ded Moroz as the native Slavs referred to him.

As the centuries passed, Grandfather Frost began to more closely resemble Saint Nicholas and Father Christmas. He wore heavy winter coats lined with white fur, although the coats were originally blue owing to the fact that this color is (quite literally) the "color of cold" in climates with more extreme wintery conditions. Even the landscapes of Scandinavian and Slavic countries, especially as one approaches the Arctic circle, take on a bluish hue. Mountains and lakes are literally blue in color because of atmospheric conditions caused by very low temperatures. This is germane to the character of Grandfather Frost since he is, in ancient mythology and accompanying depictions of his form, the personification of winter—a spirit of ice and snow. It was natural that the evolution of Morozko into Ded Moroz (Grandfather Frost) included garments that reflected the atmosphere and cold temperatures, resulting in blue coats instead of the traditional bright red clothing worn by Santa Claus.

But modern civilization, travel, rapid communication, and media have made the world a smaller place, one in which cultural influences cross-pollinate each other. In the case of Grandfather Frost, he eventually became a man usually (not always) dressed in the traditional red garments worn by the Western Santa Claus. He is now a figure that in no way resembles the ice demon Morozko. He is a kindly man who delivers presents to children at Christmastime, and he is as jovial and friendly as any Santa one might see in the United States or Europe.

This doesn't mean he is an exact carbon copy, however, of the Saint Nick who slides down chimneys and lives at the North Pole. Ded Moroz travels in a troika, which is a sleigh pulled by three white horses (white symbolizing snow and winter much as the color blue). The three horses represent the three coldest months of winter. But the greatest deviation from the common mythology of Santa Claus was caused by the Russian Revolution, also called the Bolshevik Revolution of 1917. Following the communist takeover of the country and the murder of the czar (ironically called Nicholas) and his family, Ded Moroz was outlawed because he was too closely aligned with Christianity and religion in general. Children, in fact, almost revered Grandfather Frost as a god, and gods were not allowed under the harsh, pragmatic rule of the emerging communist government. Additionally, Grandfather Frost was a bringer of toys and gifts, and this smacked of capitalism, the kind practiced by the bourgeois class in the West. Although he was honored in private homes, the public acknowledgement of Ded Moroz was banned, and for almost thirty years the Russian Santa Claus disappeared.

Years later, dictator Joseph Stalin allowed the legend of Ded Moroz to be resurrected in order to gain larger support among the commoners of Russia—the proletariat—and the Eastern block countries that, together with Mother Russia, came to be called the Soviet Union. But there were limits to how much Grandfather Frost could be celebrated. He could still be a gift-giver, but he could only deliver presents on New Year's Eve since the celebration of Christmas was strictly forbidden in the U.S.S.R. The new Soviet regime also insisted that Ded Moroz's coat be blue, as before, since a Santa wearing a red suit was too similar to the Santa in Western civilization.

Finally, it is said that Santa (and all of his incarnations) always knows whether children are naughty or nice. During the Soviet years, some people secretly joked that Santa did indeed know exactly whether people were good or bad thanks to Big Brother and the KGB, which seemed to be listening to people's conversations everywhere and spying on their activities. The party line was that Ded Moroz would only bring presents to those individuals who worked hard in conformity to acceptable Communist behavior.

Even though prohibitions against the celebration of Christmas were lifted after the fall of Berlin Wall and the overthrow of the Soviet Union in 1991, it was established that the home of Ded Moroz was not the North Pole, but rather in a home in the town of Veliky Ustyug. Despite this minor aberration, Christmas was once again celebrated in Russia and other former Soviet block countries, such as Bulgaria, Poland, and Romania. In fact, Grandfather Frost could again wear his familiar red suit and act as jolly as he wanted, That having been said, he still, more often than not, delivered presents on New Year's Eve. This date, however, was now more variable and depended on the preferences of individuals families. For some, Grandfather Frost was simply Santa Claus, the man in the red suit who came on Christmas Eve and delivered presents to the good children of Russia. In fact, with the Westernization of Russia following the collapse of the Soviet Union, Grandfather Frost was even imagined to be flying in a sleigh pulled by reindeer even though most citizens envisioned him to travel in his horse-drawn troika.

The evolution of Grandfather Frost into a more Western version of Santa demonstrates how deeply-rooted the custom is of a gift-bringer at Christmastime or New Years. The fact that the legend of an ice demon thousands of years ago eventually morphed into a man in a traditional Santa suit, one who survived communism and its harsh prohibitions against Christmas and religion, is a testament to the enduring legacy of Bishop Nicholas of Myra.

CHAPTER SEVEN
More Variations on a Common Theme

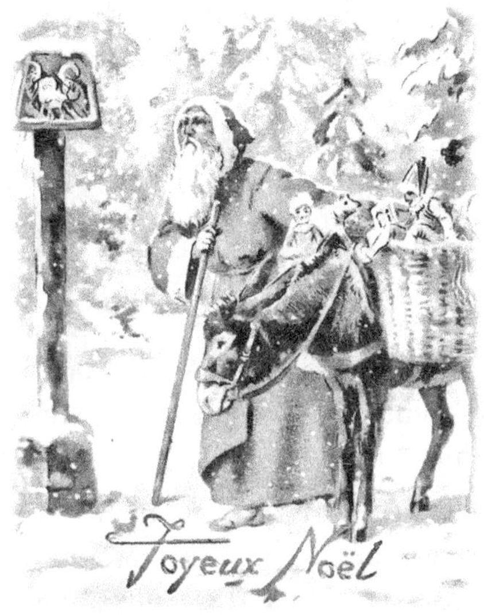

Pere Noel and Papa Noel, the names for Santa in France and Latin America, both translate as Father Christmas. In Scotland, he is the Abbot of Unreason, in China he is Dun Che Lao Ren, and in Lithuania he is Kaledu Senelis. In this chapter you'll learn many more names and traditions of Santa. Can you guess how many there are?

Thus far we have seen several figures that bear a striking resemblance to the American Santa Claus. Indeed, we have seen the evolution of Bishop Nicholas of Myra into Saint Nicholas, Father Christmas, Sinterklaas, Samichlaus, and Grandfather Frost. In all of these characterizations of the personification of Christmas, the similarities have outweighed the differences, although Grandfather Frost originally had a distinctiveness about him not shared by the others.

Santa, of course, can legitimately be called a worldwide figure and is recognizable by nearly everyone, especially young children. There is no doubt that Santa is an iconic figure, but it is probably best to categorize Santa Claus along a wide continuum that ranges from the very familiar portrait of the legendary bringer of gifts to figures that don't resemble him at all and may not bear his name or even be human, as was the case with Starman and The Little Angel. As we'll see, most fall somewhere in the middle of the continuum because of the Westernization of the Christmas holiday.

Noel is a word that literally means Christmas. In ancient times, the Latin phrase natales dies meant "the day of birth." Two thousand years ago, the Roman Empire extended to Palestine and the Holy Land, where Christ was born. Keeping in mind that tens of thousands of words in languages such as English, French, Spanish, and Italian are derived from Latin roots, this Latin phrase was shortened in French to simply nael, which meant "born on Christmas Day." In Middle English, however, which borrowed many French words thanks to the Normandy Invasion of 1066, nael became nowel. When Middle English (spoken in England at the time of the European Renaissance) evolved into modern English, spelling was modernized, and nowel became noel. Eventually, the word "noel" was capitalized and meant "Christmas" in Romance Languages, meaning all Western European languages that evolved mostly from Latin during Rome's colonization of so much of the continent.

The word for "father" in French is pere, while the word for "father" in Spanish is papa or papai. Pere Noel, therefore, literally means Father Christmas, as does Papa Noel or Papai Noel. In France and other French-speaking countries, Pere Noel is quite similar to the traditional Santa, and his appearance and attire are essentially the same as Santa's, although he looks more like Father Christmas and Saint Nicholas than the rotund, red-cheeked Santa that Coca-Cola has made famous.

Instead of milk and cookies, children leave carrots in their shoes before they go to bed on Christmas Eve. The carrots are for Gui, the donkey on which Pere Noel rides. Because Pere Noel hearkens from the slightly older traditions of Father Christmas or Saint Nicholas, he was never envisioned by the French as airborne even though he retains a certain amount of mystery when it comes to his home—is it the North Pole or is it Lapland, the northernmost portion of Finland?—and how he manages to visit all the French-speaking homes of the world in one night. The presents he brings to children, however, are usually much smaller than those Santa brings to kids in the United States. Pere Noel brings very small toys and candy that can fit into shoes, although affluent French families will nevertheless leave more lavish presents underneath their Christmas trees as they help Pere Noel fulfill his yearly mission.

In Southeastern Louisiana, Pere Noel is celebrated widely since New Orleans and most of the Mississippi delta was originally colonized by French and Spanish settlers. The phrase Merry Christmas is often translated as Joyeux Noel. In Cajun country—the bayous surrounding the Mississippi River—Pere Noel does indeed ride a sleigh and is guided to the homes of children by enormous bonfires built atop the levee system that guards New Orleans and nearby cities from floods and hurricanes. A variation of this tradition is that Pere Noel travels in a pirogue pulled by eight alligators (substitutes for reindeer) as he travels the swamps in order to reach Cajun homes along Louisiana's many waterways.

Hispanic culture is far more diverse in how Santa Claus is portrayed, and for many centuries he wasn't acknowledged at all in most Spanish-speaking countries. Today, Papa Noel (or Papai Noel, as he is called in Brazil) is a prominent figure in the celebration of Christmas in Hispanic culture, which includes Spain as well as countries in Latin and Central America. He is a red-clad man who usually travels by sleigh on Christmas Eve and operates more or less according to the Western traditions surrounding Santa Claus. This is due to the spread of the legend of Santa in the twentieth and twenty-first centuries. His image and mythology spread even faster when the digital age brought a common body of information about Saint Nick to virtually every country in the world. In Latin America and Chile, he is called Viejito Pascuero, although he dresses no differently than any other Santa. In Portugal, he is called Pai Natal, which is Portuguese for Father Christmas. Depending on the country, Papa Noel may deposit small gifts in the shoes of children or may bring large presents under the family Christmas tree. The most important thing to remember is that Hispanic countries are heavily Catholic and, as such, they place a great deal of emphasis on the Nativity and birth of Christ. Because of this, Papa Noel is mostly associated with Saint Nicholas regardless of whether or not he has been Westernized to one degree or another. To be sure, he is a gift-giver, but a saintly one who is to be revered and respected.

All this having been said, Santa has a lot of competition in Hispanic culture when it comes to who "delivers the goods" at Christmastime. Competitors include Los Tres Magos (The Three Kings) and Nino Jesus (or Baby Jesus). Los Tres Magos are most popular in Spain, Uruguay, and Argentina, and they bring presents on January 6th, the Feast of the Epiphany, which celebrates The Wise Men bringing gifts to Christ in the manger. Often, the gifts are left on January 5th, the eve of the Feast of the Epiphany. The Baby Jesus delivers gifts on December 24th, and Niño Jesus is most commonly regarded as the gift-giver in Colombia, Venezuela, Peru, and Bolivia.

*   *   *

Thus far, we've been discussing Christmas gift-givers who strongly resemble the Western Santa Claus. Other countries carry on the traditions already described, but the origin of their Santas is a bit more complex. In Lithuania, for example, Santa Claus is called Kaledu Senelis. He is most often depicted as a jolly fat man with a long white beard and dressed in red. In fact, his entire image is quite Western since he drives a sleigh pulled by reindeer and lives at the North Pole. The Lithuanian belief in this well-recognized figure stems from many sources. Christians in this country strongly identified Christmas with Bishop Nicholas of Myra, Father Christmas, and Saint Nicholas, who they called Saint Mikalojus. Ironically Saint Mikalojus has more in common with Bishop Nicholas than his offshoots. Saint Mikalojus, for example, is the patron saint of children, sailors, archers, and prostitutes. If you recall, Bishop Nicholas paid the dowry for a father's daughters so that they could be married and spared a life of prostitution.

But the Lithuanian Santa also derives from much older Germanic legends of Norse mythology. One of the more prominent figures in these pagan Norse myths is Odin, called Wotan in Old English. Odin was described in Norse tales as an old man with a white beard who carried a staff and wore a floppy hat. While this may not be the man we see riding the last float of the Macy's Parade at Thanksgiving, the basic elements of Santa's dress are intact. But the similarity to Santa goes even deeper when his full mythology is examined. Odin would go on a yearly hunt at the time of the winter solstice. Because Odin rode a flying horse (think reindeer!) named Slepnir, children would leave sugar, straw, and carrots for the horse, and in a spirit of gratitude, the Norse god would leave candy and sweets by the fireplaces of those homes who chose to help Odin and Slepnir on their hunt. The fireplace, of course, is central to the yearly mission of Santa Claus. When all of these various elements of Norse myth are added to that of Saint Mikalojus, the result is a conflated figure who is, for all intents and purposes, the man we call Saint Nick, or Santa Claus.

*   *   *

Aussie Santa is the Santa Claus in Australia and has a distinctive Down Under flavor. The legend of Santa is certainly known in Australia, but Santa more often than not drives a jeep and wears the outfit of a cattleman or rancher since Christmas below the equator falls in the middle of summer. As far as legend goes, Aussie Santa, as he is known, rides in a sleigh pulled by kangaroos, with baby kangaroos in their mothers' pouches acting as Santa's helpers in distributing gifts. He gives gifts to children and adults, but no milk and cookies are left out to help Santa on his way. In Australia, they leave beer! The Aussies have a unique kind of Christmas celebration, which includes barbecues and trips to the beach. Santa is apparently as laidback about the whole holiday as anyone else.

Speaking of beer, in Ireland Santa Claus is called Daidi na Nollog, which translates from Gaelic (the native language of Ireland before it was assimilated into the United Kingdom) into Father Christmas. He is the traditional Santa who drives a sleigh, but on Christmas Eve, children leave carrots for the reindeer and beer for Santa instead of sweets or milk. In grand Irish tradition, Santa must be quite tipsy when he finishes his rounds and arrives at the North Pole. As some Irish say, it's a good thing Santa has Rudolph to guide the sleigh since Santa might not be capable of driving by the end of the night.

Christmas is not a big holiday in China, although with more and more Western culture leeching into the country, not to mention American businesses, the celebration is not completely contained by the repressive communist Chinese government. People who celebrate the holiday tend to do so on the downlow, although holiday lights can be seen in some parts of the country. These are referred to as New Year's lights, however, since Christianity is not sanctioned by the communist regime. But where there is Christmas there is always—somehow, some way—a Santa Claus. In China he is known as Dun Che Lao Ren, which means Christmas Old Man. Children hang muslin stocking in their homes, usually on the mantel by the fireplace, in the hopes that Christmas Old Man will leave them some candy. Because of growing commercialism, China has taken a more lenient stand when it comes to department stores decorating their windows and offering Christmas specials. And who else but Dun Che Lao Ren is featured in these displays, wearing the traditional red Santa costume? China apparently turns its bureaucratic eye away from such displays, including some Christmas Eve dinners offered at fancy restaurants, when profit enters the picture.

In Mongolia and other parts of China, the Santa equivalent is called Tasi Shen Yeh (also known as Zhang Gong Ming). He is the god of wealth and is depicted as riding a tiger. He is considered to be a variant of Saint Nicholas inasmuch as folklore claims that he showered children with money and small toys. This usually took place on or near New Year's, which was also a time when nomadic herdsman had what we would call a rodeo in the West. For the affluent in Chinese or Mongolian culture, Tsai Shen Yeh is sometimes dressed as any other Western Santa Claus, although he sometimes wears a leather or rope cinch around his waist instead of the familiar wide black belt, and his boots may be tall and furry, similar to the ones worn by Mongol nomads. Likewise, his hat may be a simple brown fur cap. In these respects, Tsai Shen Yeh is truly a hybrid Santa that combines modern Santa tradition with Chinese mythology and religion, which contains a pantheon of several hundred gods and goddesses.

In some areas of Mongolia, Santa is called Grandpa of Winter, and he is dressed like most conventional Santa Clauses who are modeled on Saint Nicholas. A variation of Grandpa of Winter is Mongol Winter Grandpa, who is dressed more like a soldier, although he has a white beard and wears warm and colorful fur garments. He is often portrayed carrying a staff with a star on top.

In Korea, Santa is called Sana Haraboji. He is equated with the Western Santa Claus by many South Koreans, who view the Christmas season as a time to party since Christianity, while present in Korea, is not the prevalent religion. Sana Haraboji is often a short man dressed in a green hat and warm suit, causing some to compare him to an Irish Christmas elf.

*   *   *

We have already discussed Christmas in the United Kingdom, where Father Christmas takes precedence over all other gift-giving figures who grace homes with presents at Christmas, often called Yuletide. In earlier days, however, Christmastime was presided over by a man called The Lord of Misrule, also called The Abbot of Unreason. Christmas celebrations orchestrated by this figure hearkened back to the orgiastic pagan days when the winter solstice was accompanied by a great deal of partying and drinking. These wild feasts, as you will recall, originated during the Roman occupation of Great Britain that began in the first century. The Romans had the same number of gods as are found in Greek mythology, only the Romans gave these colorful figures their very own names. In other words, Greek and Roman mythology are very close except in terms of nomenclature. For example, the Greek god Zeus was called Jupiter by the Romans. Dionysius, the god of pleasure and revelry, was called Bacchus in Rome. Cronus was called Saturn, who was the god of wealth, plenty, abundance, and agriculture in Rome. A feast celebrating this god and the anticipated spring harvest—once again taking place at the time of the winter solstice—was called a Saturnalia, or the Feast of Fools. These were also wild, orgiastic parties, which is why those who have studied Yuletide traditions of the United Kingdom believe that feasts presided over by the Lord of Misrule originated in the parties to honor the god Saturn.

By the sixteenth century, the Anglican Church, also called The Church of England after Henry VIII married six wives and thus broke with the Catholic religion, allowed such celebrations to take place. These were ruled by a boy dressed up as a bishop, but this custom seemed too blasphemous even for the philandering and heavy-drinking Henry VIII, who abolished pagan feasting in favor of honoring Christmas. He was, after all, under great pressure to preserve as many Catholic traditions as possible in order to claim that his church had as much legitimacy as the church in Rome. But once a tradition is started, especially one involving a great deal of mischief and partying, it's hard to put the brakes on. Although Henry VIII and Queen Elizabeth I outlawed the festivities overseen by the Lord of Misrule, they were resurrected time and again in England, Scotland, Wales, and even in some places in Europe, most notably France.

In Scotland, the figure was termed the Abbot of Unreason to try to put a bit more of a Christian spin on the partying, which was allegedly tamed quite a bit, although church leaders, both Catholic and Anglican, continued to condemn the festivities as sinful and aligned with the forces of darkness. When it comes to performing ecclesiastical duties—those of the church—an abbot usually has as much power as a bishop or an archbishop, and so the Scots thought they might be putting one over on the rest of the United Kingdom by aligning the Abbot of Unreason with Saint Nicholas who, as we have seen, was originally Bishop Nicholas of Myra. The slight change in title had little effect, however, and the quasi-pagan festivities were still condemned as sinful. Christmas, it was proclaimed, was a time to usher in the light of Christ (and of spring). Over the centuries, the people have Scotland have nevertheless incorporated the Abbot of Unreason into their holiday celebrations, and he is dressed, with some variation, much like Father Christmas. This doesn't mean that a man dressed as the Abbot of Unreason doesn't make appearances at Scottish and Irish taverns during the Christmas season. The people of Ireland and Scotland are not known for their abstinence when it comes to the consumption of strong drink.

CHAPTER EIGHT
Other Gift-Givers at Christmastime

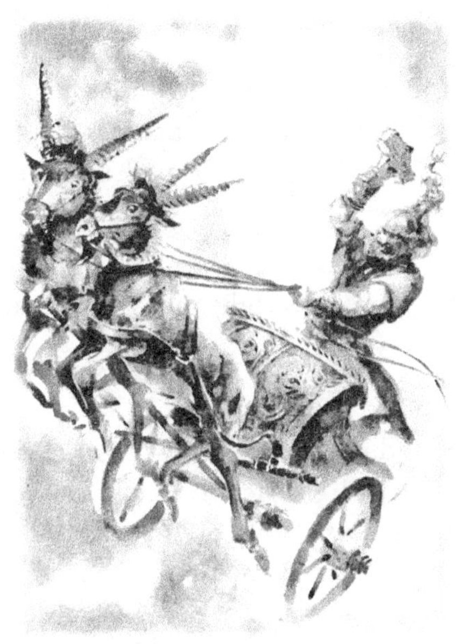

Germany and Scandinavia have very unique Santa Clauses, from Jules Venn to Joulupukki. They may ride in carriages, carts, or sleds—or even magically fly through the air—on Christmas Eve. In some parts of Scandinavia, the Yule Goat delivers presents! Today, the Yule Goat takes a back seat to Santa, but he's still an important symbol of the season.

The Yule Goat is popular in Scandinavian culture and dates back hundreds (and perhaps thousands) of years in Norse mythology. December ushers in the sign of Capricorn, or the Goat, and in pagan rituals a goat was sacrificed to the god Thor, who was believed to drive through the sky on a chariot pulled by two goats (the goats being associated with the astrological sign). Winter celebrations in Scandinavia were called Julbocken, which translates to Yule Goat. We have already seen that the word "Yule" means "the time of Christmas," although in ancient times "Yule" meant "the time of the winter solstice," or December 21st.

By the eleventh century, Scandinavia had begun to be Christianized to the extent that a Yule Goat (or someone dressed as a goat) would be led through the town at Christmastime by someone dressed as Saint Nicholas to symbolize Christ's victory over sin, evil, the devil, and the pagan rituals and sacrifices that had preceded the celebration of the Nativity. By the nineteenth century, the holiday season was so saturated by Christian culture that the Yule Goat was replaced by Father Christmas, called Jultomte. By the twentieth century, Finland and other parts of Scandinavia had replaced the Yule Goat with Santa Claus, called Joulupukki.

The lines between Joulupukki and Santa Claus are sometimes blurred. He may ride in a sleigh pulled by reindeer and fly through the sky to deliver presents, or he may travel on a sled (called a pullka) pulled through the snow by reindeer. "Rudolph the Red-Nosed Reindeer" is a popular Christmas song in Finland (reinforcing the flying version of Joulupukki), and the Finnish Santa has a Mrs. Claus counterpart, named Joulumuori. Both Mr. and Mrs. Claus wear warm red robes with white (or blue) piping. Most scholars who have studied Norse mythology and Northern European traditions maintain that it was the Christian figure of Saint Nicholas, more than anyone else, who transformed the Yule Goat into Joulupukki, or Santa Claus.

All of these figures were gift-givers, and the fact that they flew through the sky can be traced to Thor riding his chariot (sleigh) pulled by goats (reindeer).

*   *   *

In parts of Finland, Norway, other Scandinavian countries, and the tip of Northern Europe (especially Germany), the concept of a gift-giver evolved in a slightly different fashion. In Norse folklore, a nisse. also called a tomte (some traditions say that there were many nisse, so that the word may be both singular and plural), was a gnome-like figure who had a long white beard and wore a warm red coat topped by a knitted red cap. He was seen as a caretaker of animals and farms and wore farm breeches cinched at the waist. He was generally viewed as a beneficent creature unless someone harmed or cursed him. It is easy to see that even before the Christianization of these countries, a Santa Claus precursor already existed.

As Christianity expanded in this area by the Middle Ages, many bishops and priests urged their parishioner to abandon any thought or worship of these ancient creatures since they were equated by Catholicism with the devil. Over the centuries, the figure of the nisse was merged with that of Father Christmas, and the resulting image was usually called Julenisse, meaning "Christmas Spirit." Other Scandinavian traditions eventually conflated him with the Yule Goat. Twentieth century commercialization has made Julenesse look more and more like the American Santa Claus, and he indeed brings presents on Christmas Eve via sleigh and reindeer.

In parts of Norway, a slight variation on Julenesse is Julesvenn. Julesvenn (or Jules Venn) was an ancient Norse character who would appear in people's homes during the winter solstice for the purpose of hiding good luck barley sticks around the home and village. He, too, was a gnome-like figure, one dressed similarly to Julesnesse or a tomte. His magical appearance inside a home obviously resembles Santa's mysterious appearance in homes around the world.

Most Scandinavian traditions regarding Christmas and Santa Claus (and his pagan equivalents) are quite similar given the strong cultural bonds shared among Norway, Sweden, Finland, and Denmark.

Iceland was settled by the Vikings over the course of many centuries as they sailed, not only to Iceland, but also to various spots along the coast of what is now Newfoundland and perhaps as far south as Maine. The Santa substitute in Iceland is called Jola Sveinar, known in English as The Yule Lads. These twelve figures (sometimes thirteen) are short dwarf-like beings (or trolls) with faces that have exaggerated—even grotesque—features. Beginning on December 12th, children who believe in The Yule Lads will put shoes on their windowsills in the hopes that one of the lads will deposit a present in them. The Yule Lads, originally quite mischievous, were often thought to steal food from the homes they visited, but in more modern times they are thirteen Santa Clauses who visit the homes of children. Their mother is Gryla, a fearsome gremlin who was believed to leave her mountain home at Christmas in order to boil naughty children. In Gryla is that element of the Santa tradition that says naughty children do not get presents and, to the contrary, are often punished, in this case quite harshly.

The names of The Yule Lads are Sheep Cote Clod, Gully Gawk, Stubby, Spoon Licker, Pot Licker, Bowl Licker, Door Slammer, Skyr Gobbler, Sausage Swiper, Window Peeper, Doorway Sniffer, Meat Hook, and Candle Stealer. As is easily seen, these names do not connote friendly beings and resemble some of the scarier legends of their forebears, the nisse. Today, however, children are not afraid of these odd characters. Rather, they anticipate their arrival in the days leading up to Christmas since the lads are bearers of gifts.

Part Two
Santa Substitutes

CHAPTER NINE
The Magi

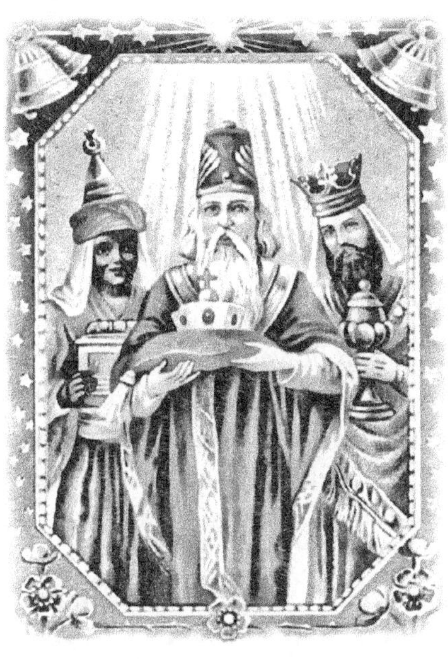

The Magi are The Three Wise Men who traveled from Persia to deliver gold, frankincense, and myrrh to the Christ Child. These Zoroastrian high priests journeyed to Palestine after seeing the Christmas star. They are considered by devout Christians as the original givers of gifts at Christmastime, and they are celebrated on January 6th, the Feast of the Epiphany.

In the Middle East, Santa is called Holy Man, usually an ancient king who brought gifts to his people. Most students of Christmas traditions believe that Holy Man is not a single man, but three, namely The Magi, also called The Three Kings or The Three Wise Men. We have already seen that certain Spanish-speaking cultures put more of a premium on The Magi—called Los Tres Magos—than they do on Santa Claus even if the jolly man has found his way into Hispanic Christmas traditions. In fact, many countries around the world place far more emphasis on the Feast of the Epiphany, celebrated on January 6th, than on Christmas Eve, Christmas Day, or Santa Claus. Even if Santa delivers some of the expected presents on Christmas Eve, many believe the Epiphany is the real day for receiving or exchanging presents, and this emphasis extends far beyond Latin countries.

In such countries, the Epiphany is of greater importance because it is the celebration of The Wise Men delivering presents to the Christ Child in the manger. It is called the Epiphany because the discovery of a newborn king—Christ the Lord—was a revelation and the beginning of a new period in religious history, one that would forever change virtually every civilization around the world regardless of whether or not it was Christian. The reality, however, is that The Magi probably did not find Christ until he was three or four years old, at which time he was living in

Nazareth with his earthly parents, Mary and Joseph. The term "magi" is plural for "magus," a term that literally means king, magician, or sorcerer. A magus was believed to possess certain abilities beyond those of ordinary men and women, an individual (always male) who was an avatar of sorts and an intermediary between average people and the gods.

At this point, it is necessary to briefly summarize the story of The Magi in order to show how they are connected to the legend of Santa Claus, and believe it or not, there is indeed a strong connection. It is believed by Roman and Jewish historians writing in Palestine two thousand years ago that The Magi were real people, not inventions of the men who wrote the Christian gospels. Early Jewish and Roman narratives describe these three figures as kings from various provinces in Persia, now modern-day Iran. They were probably also astrologers who followed the religion called Zoroastrianism. Zoroaster was a supreme god in this Persian faith, which was characterized by two important tenets: there is a single, all-knowing god, and that good will ultimately conquer evil. This meshed perfectly with the core beliefs of Judaism two thousand years ago. The Magi were also, according to legends of the time, astrologers who consulted the heavens for signs as to what might be expected on Earth in this fight of good against evil.

As the Bible attests, these three kings saw a new star appear rather suddenly in the heavens, one that seemed to move and point to a specific geographical location to their west. Twentieth century scientists believe that the Christmas star was quite real and have offered two theories to support this astronomical claim. The Christmas star may have been a supernova, which is the explosion of a massive red giant star. When a giant star explodes, it shines so brightly that it can be seen across the entire galaxy (or even in neighboring galaxies) and outshines all other celestial objects, including the moon, for a number of days and may be visible for months or even years. The remnants of a supernova in the constellation Centaurus were discovered by ancient Chinese astronomers in the year 185 A.D., but the operative word here is "remnants." A supernova sends out much light, but also gas and debris that form a colorful nebula extending many light years from the original explosion. In other words, what the Chinese say would tally perfectly with an explosion that occurred at the time of Christ. Since the heavenly stars move above our heads nightly as the Earth spins, the supernova would likewise appear to be moving, causing some to think that it was leading The Magi to Palestine.

Another theory, and one just as likely to be true, also comes from reliable Chinese astronomical observations of what modern scientists believe was a comet that appeared in the constellation of Capricorn in 5 B.C. The long tail of the comet may well have been angled in such a way so that it pointed towards the town of Bethlehem. In the fourteenth century, the Italian artist Giotto painted a nativity scene in which a comet points to the manger below, with the Christ Child being worshipped by The Three Wise Men. It is not known whether Giotto knew of the Chinese astronomical observation mentioned above, although trade between the Orient and the West had been established by the fourteenth century, and knowledge of such a portent in the sky would likely have been carried from China to Italy.

But what of the story of The Magi as it is written in the Gospel of Matthew? The pertinent details are that The Magi saw a great star in the sky and set off from their homeland to pay tribute to the new king. Upon arriving in Judea in Palestine, they stopped and asked Herod Antipas, the tetrarch of Judea, where to find the newborn king. King Herod was alarmed by their request, although his own astrologers, according to some accounts, had also seen a sign in the heavens. Fearing that a new king might one day rival his own reign over the Roman province of Judea, he ordered The Magi to find the new king and report back to him when they had located "the Christ" so that he, too, might visit and adore this new ruler. In actuality, he wanted to know the location of the birth so that he could kill the Christ Child and thus crush any future claimant to his throne. The Wise Men, the gospel tells us, were warned in a dream to secretly return home by a different route and not warn Herod of the child they had found so that the tetrarch would not kill Jesus. And this is what they did. When Herod found out that he had been deceived, he was enraged and ordered all children two years old and younger to be killed. This is known as The Slaughter of the Holy Innocents. He couldn't be sure of when the new king had been born, so he decided on age two as a cutoff point in order to be sure to kill Christ in case he had been born (as was really the case) before The Wise Men arrived in his country. Later, Joseph was warned in a dream that he was to take the Infant Jesus to Egypt until the danger to Christ had passed and Herod was dead. He took Mary and Jesus to Egypt, therefore, and returned a few years later when another dream assured him that it was safe to return to Palestine.

The Three Wise Men were given names according to ancient texts that date back as far as the first century, including the Dead Sea Scrolls and other gospels describing the life of Jesus (such as the Gospel of Thomas) that were not included in the final version of the New Testament (which was declared to be the official cannon of the Church by various church councils in the fourth century). Their names were Caspar, Melchior, and Balthazar. It was written that Caspar gave gold to the Christ Child, while Melchior gave frankincense, and Balthazar gave myrrh. Frankincense and myrrh are aromatic herbs that are used for both cooking and healing. In the ancient world, these two herbs were both rare and expensive and therefore considered fit for a king. These latter two gifts also exist in the form of an oil and were often used to anoint kings and high priests. In the folklore of the time, all three gifts represented the concept of kingship.

Biblical scholars are divided as to how historically accurate these early texts were, and some have claimed that the idea of three kings bowing down before a savior and offering him gifts was originally mentioned in chapter sixty of the Book of Isaiah as well as Psalm 72. Both of these Old Testament books would have been known to the gospel writers. Whether one believes the kings to be mythical or the result of research into Roman and Jewish history as well as the Dead Sea Scrolls, the story of The Magi is part of what are called the Infancy Narratives in the gospels of Matthew and Luke, and therefore the kings became an integral part of Christmas celebrations centuries ago.

For this reason, countries with a higher percentage of Christians, especially Catholics, have placed a far greater emphasis on the Feast of the Epiphany as the time to give gifts rather than on Christmas Day, which for many who practice the faith year-round by attending church is the proper way to display generosity while avoiding the commercialization of the holiday season. It is in these countries and among these Christians that we find a connection to Santa Claus. The Magi were the original bringers of valuable gifts. Also, the three priests were allegedly dressed in colorful royal robes and wore crowns, and while such attire and accoutrements do not constitute a Santa suit, many believe that Santa wears his traditional colorful clothing not just to keep warm but to honor the true spirit of the season. The Wise Men traveled by camel caravan to Bethlehem, and therefore they engaged in a long journey in order deliver their precious gifts to Christ. Santa, of course, makes quite a long journey each year to deliver his own payload of precious cargo. While The Magi certainly did not fly, many have pointed out that Santa supposedly guides his movements by using the stars as reference points. In fact, each year, NORAD (the North American Aerospace Command) is said to monitor the heavenly movements of Santa as he journeys from country to country, hemisphere to hemisphere. And it goes without saying that The Three Wise Men gave their presents to a very young child (regardless of whether he was an infant or a slightly older child, as most historians claim) just as Santa primarily gives his presents to the children of the world. While these comparisons may seem arbitrary, the parallels are clearly present. It is therefore not surprising that so many people around the world believe that The Magi more than fulfill the role of Santa Claus.

And yet there is an historical footnote that may link Santa Claus to The Magi in an even stronger way. There are those church historians who believe that Bishop Nicholas of Myra, upon whom so much Santa folklore depends and who was quite literally the man we call Saint Nicholas, was himself inspired, as a Christian bishop, to give gifts as a way of emulating the gift-giving of the Three Wise Men. This may be apocryphal, but it is known with surety that Nicholas, both as a young boy and as a bishop, diligently studied the writings of the New Testament and therefore would have been more than passingly familiar with the part that The Magi played in the Nativity. Furthermore, Bishop Nicholas named his horse North Star since the North Star (known by astronomers as Polaris) was known to guide so many travelers to their destination. The correspondence between the North Star and the Christmas Star is obvious, both stars functioning as a heavenly way to find one's path in the night to a point of illumination, whether that point is called "home" or the Christ Child, who would later proclaim himself the Light of the World.

The question remains: can The Magi legitimately and collectively be classified as a Santa Claus? You've read the chapter, so I'll let you, the reader, be the judge. Just remember that Christmas is a season of magic, a time when anything is possible. By the way, the word "magic" is derived from the Greek word magoi, which refers to the sorcery and rituals practiced by the high priests of Zoroastrianism in Persia—in other words, men who were called "magi."

*　　　*　　　*

In Italy, the figure of Befana is strongly linked to The Three Wise Men, and it is she who delivers presents on the eve of the Epiphany. Her name derives from the Italian phrase for the Feast of the Epiphany, which is Festa dell'Epifania. One can easily see the similarity between the words Epifania (epiphany) and Befana. She is portrayed as an ugly hag dressed in a black dress and shawl, and she rides a broomstick from house to house, stopping at each one to slide down the chimney in order to fill the socks and stockings of children with candy and presents if they have been good, while giving them lumps of coal if they've been bad. Instead of milk and cookies, parents leave a glass of wine out for Befana in the hopes that she will be kind to the household.

La Befana has an even deeper connection to The Magi. The legend of Befana says that The Three Wise Men stopped at Befana's humble abode a few days before they arrived at the manger where the Christ Child was born. Because they did not yet know the precise location where the birth was to take place, they asked Befana if she could tell them where the new king was to be born because they had seen his sign rise in the sky: a new star that had previously not been on their charts. She told them that she did not know where the event was to take place, but she invited them in and gave them shelter for the night. The next morning, the royal Persian astrologers asked her if she wished to join them on their journey to honor the new king, but she declined. Shortly thereafter, the legend says, she had a change of heart and set off to find The Wise Men, but they were nowhere to be found. It is said that she is still searching for the Baby Jesus, and as she travels she leaves candy and presents at the homes of children who have behaved themselves.

A variation of this myth states that Befana was a fastidious housekeeper who did nothing from dawn to dusk except clean her home. In fact, she was so busy cleaning one day that she actually turned away The Magi because she was consumed with her daily chores. She changed her mind the next day and set off looking for the kings and the Infant Jesus, following a bright star in the sky that was presumably the Christmas

Star, the same star by which the kings themselves had found their way to Palestine. She brought along a sack of food—mostly baked goods and breads—for the new king as well as a broom so that Jesus' mother Mary could sweep her home, Befana believing that a new king should naturally live in a clean home, just as she. She never found the Messiah but is still searching for the Christ Child all these centuries later. As she continues her search, she stops at the home of children and leaves them presents and food.

There is yet another variation on the myth of Befana that states that she was a village woman who had given birth to a baby who died soon after the delivery. In her grief, Befana went insane. When she heard a rumor that Jesus had been born, she set out to find him, believing in her maddened state that he was in reality her own son. When she found Jesus, the newborn infant king was so touched by her perseverance in finding him that he gave her a unique gift in return for her trouble, which was that she was to be the mother of all children in Italy, a mother who would deliver presents to them each and every year.

These are all endearing tales of a woman who had intimate and direct contact with either The Magi or Christ himself. However one interprets these myths, one can plainly see that Befana is one of many Santa substitutes that legend has produced over the years, one that retains the basic traditions and spirit of gift-giving at Christmastime.

CHAPTER TEN
Christkindl and Kris Kringle

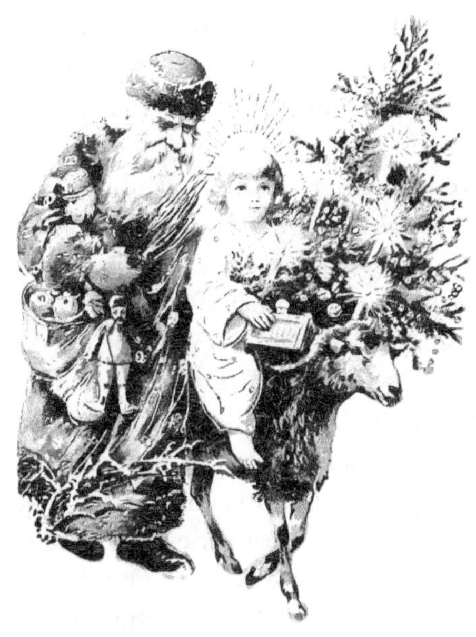

Martin Luther started the Protestant Reformation in the Middle Ages, and he was not a fan of Christmas at all—or of Santa, who he believed detracted from the true meaning of Christmas. Santa was therefore replaced by the Christ Child, called the Christkindl in German, who supposedly descended from the heavens to deliver presents in person on Christmas Eve.

Christmas traditions relating to Santa, as well as the way Christmas was celebrated in general, changed radically in sixteenth century Europe when Martin Luther began the Protestant Reformation after Luther nailed his Ninety-Five Theses to the cathedral door in Wittenberg, Germany. Luther was essentially breaking with the papal authority of the Catholic Church, which he deemed false and corrupt as evidenced by the many corrupt people of the Middle Ages, such as the Medici and the Borgia families, who had sought political power and wealth while overseeing the church from Rome. Many popes had mistresses and numerous children. Most of all, Luther objected to the growing Catholic tradition of selling indulgences, which meant that people could sin and then pay for them monetarily and thus avoid spending time in purgatory. This was the beginning of the Lutheran Church and many other reformed churches in Europe, all of which disputed the pope's power.

Luther was especially disturbed by the way Christians celebrated Christmas. Just as many Christians in modern times have objected to the commercialization of Christmas, Luther thought that the emphasis on Saint Nicholas was inappropriate. Saint Nick was bringing gifts to children, and although he had been proclaimed a saint by the Catholic Church based on the canonization of Bishop Nicholas of Myra, Luther believed that the emphasis of Christmas had been radically misplaced from the birth of Christ to a man who traveled the world to deliver toys. People anticipated receiving toys during the holiday season as opposed to receiving Christ into their hearts.

The Protestant Reformation (the word Protestant" deriving from the word "protest") therefore declared that it was the Christ Child himself, known as Christkindl in German, who was the bringer of Christmas gifts. The name is alternately spelled "Christkind" depending on the exact region where this tradition was honored. Furthermore, the date that the Christkindl would deliver his gifts would be on Christmas Eve so as to detract attention from the Feast of Saint Nicholas on December 6th. Ironically, this mindset was adopted by many who decided to remain in the Catholic Church because the sentiment seemed appropriate given the original biblical events behind the entire reason for celebrating Christmas. This attitude towards gift-giving spread to many Hispanic cultures as well as many countries in Eastern Europe. One need only call to mind the millions of bumper stickers and yard signs displayed each year that say KEEP CHRIST IN CHRISTMAS. Although many countries had already shifted their emphasis from Santa Claus to the Three Wise Men in terms of the dispensing of presents, proclaiming the Christ Child as the bringer of good things at Christmastime seemed even more appropriate and more in sync with biblical narratives of the Nativity.

But to actually imagine Christ himself as the person who would deposit presents in people's homes was a bit of a stretch, and as the Reformation continued in Europe, the Christkindl was perceived to be a sprite of sorts, a very small child with angelic wings and blond hair, this representation attempting to merge the Infant Jesus born in Bethlehem with a being who could fly and somehow magically bring gifts to the world on a single night, that being Christmas Eve. It was an amalgamation that the Reformation could live with, and the belief that the Christkindl delivered gifts spread to most parts of Germany as well as Austria, Switzerland, Luxembourg, Belgium, Poland, Hungary, and those parts of Eastern Europe now known as the Czech Republic, Serbia, Croatia, and Slovakia. The Christkindl also became the gift-giver for Portugal and parts of Central and South America. The Christkindl is also popular in Acadiana, which is the French-speaking Cajun region of Louisiana. In other Latin countries, he is called Niño Jesus or Niño Dios. In Eastern European countries, the name is closer to that of Jesus.

In the Czech Republic, Hungary, and Slovakia, for example, he is called, respectively, Jezisek, Jezuska, and Jezisko.

In most countries in which the Christkindl is believed to deliver presents (regardless of how his name is spelled), the tradition is that parents usher their children into the living room—or wherever the Christmas tree is located—and tell their children that they may not see the angelic Christkindl and that it is bad luck to try to spot him. A family member, therefore, rings a bell to signal that the Christkindl has left the home and that it is now safe to inspect the presents under the tree. In some countries, the Chriskindl is thought to deliver not only presents but also the tree and all household Christmas decorations—sometimes even food.

In art, Jezisek, Jezuska, and Jezisko are often depicted as a very young child—perhaps age two or three—rather than an angelic spirit who comes in the form of a child. Furthermore, it is thought that the Christkindl gave birth to the icon named the Infant Jesus of Prague, Prague being the capital of the former Czechoslovakia. This statue of the Infant Jesus is honored mostly at Christmastime, and the figure wears robes and Christian canonical vestments similar to those of a bishop. The Infant Jesus of Prague also wears a crown and holds in one of his hands a globe topped by a cross, called the globus cruciger. It is ironic that we once again arrive at the image of gift-giver wearing the outfit of a bishop not unlike that worn by Bishop Nicholas or his saintly counterpart, Saint Nicholas.

In Cajun country in Louisiana, the Christkindl is called La Christiane, and this angelic figure representing the Christ Child delivers bread, fruit, and candies, mostly homemade. In more recent times, La Christiane is thought to accompany Papa Noel on his Christmas Eve journey, while other accounts name her as Mrs. Claus.

It is worth noticing that the legend of the Christkindl echoes The Little Angel that was mentioned in the chapter on Samichlaus. If you recall, The Little Angel was believed to be the gift-giver rather than Samichlaus or, in some cases, thought to be his helper or even travel with him.

It seems that no matter how local traditions affect the image of a Christmas benefactor, one who rewards good children for their deeds during the year, Santa Claus remains an enduring figure and eventually supplants local folklore or, at the very least, manages to either coexist with the legend or merge with the pre-existing tradition. This latter point is exemplified most clearly in the fact that Santa is often called Kris Kringle. This appellation derives from a Pennsylvania- German variation on the spelling of Christkindl. As German and English spellings began to produce a more American vernacular for various expressions, Christkindl morphed into Kris Kringle in the nineteenth century. In American folk art, Kris Kringle was viewed more as Santa Claus than an infant angel or Baby Jesus. The name is now synonymous with Santa Claus, and this is evident in modern American in the movie Miracle on 34th Street. The department store Santa who claims to be the real Santa calls himself Kris, although it is not until later in the film that his full identity is revealed as Kris Kringle, or Santa Claus. Were it not for Martin Luther and the Protestant Reformation, there would have been no Christkindl, and without the Christkindl there may never have been a film called Miracle on 34th Street.

Even if one does not believe in flying reindeer, a sleigh, and Santa headquarters at the North Pole, it's hard for anyone to deny that Santa is real when one considers all of the traditions that have grown out of the Nativity, The Magi, and Bishop Nicholas of Myra. These are real events and people, and that's something that can't be disputed. The rest, as they say, is history.

Part Three
Santa's Helpers

CHAPTER ELEVEN
Mrs. Claus

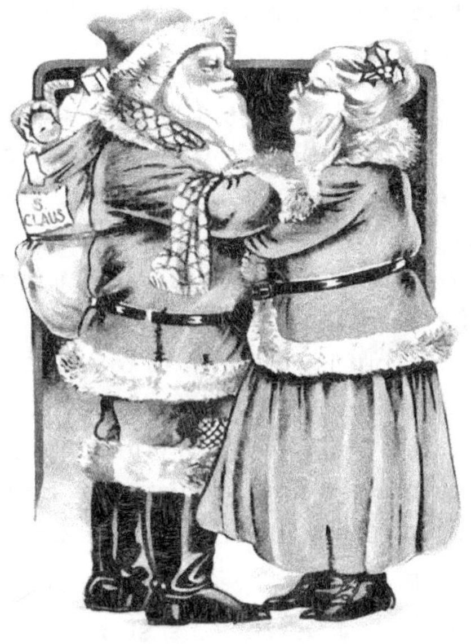

What would Christmas be without Mrs. Claus? Her legend began with only a few short stories published in magazines in the nineteenth century. Her image and importance grew over the years, and now she helps keep things tidy at the North Pole. Nobody wants Santa to be lonely, right?

Mrs. Claus has become almost as important as Santa himself, and as such, she is regarded as his chief helper. As we shall see, in some legends of Santa Claus, she actually carries out his duties if he is not available, perhaps because he's not feeling well. In other legends, she accompanies Santa on his yearly journey. Her mythology has grown over the centuries, and nowadays it is hard to conceive of the traditional version of Santa, both in the United States and other countries around the world that have adopted the more Americanized version of Saint Nick, without including Mrs. Claus as his chief companion at the North Pole.

Are there any historical accounts that would cause anyone to believe that Mrs. Claus has a basis in reality? Not really. Bishop Nicholas of Myra never married since the Catholic Church, by the fourth century, had prohibited clergy members from marrying, and enough is known about his life to confirm that Nicholas never had a wife. That having been said, documents dating back to sixteenth century England mention that Father Christmas—the more popular name for Santa in the United Kingdom, if you recall—had a lawful Christian wife. It is said that Mr. and Mrs. Yule would ride through the streets of York, England, in a carriage with the mayor to usher in Christmas season on the Feast of Saint Thomas, which is celebrated anywhere between October 6th and December 21st. The couple carried bread and a leg of lamb to give to the people. The local archbishop put an end to this annual parade because he believed it detracted from the holiness of the season. It is not known how the belief originated that Father Christmas had a wife, and the belief may have been localized to the town of York. Suffice to say that some people in England thought it quite natural that Father Christmas have a Christian companion in the form of a wife.

Fast forward several centuries, and Mrs. Claus was eventually portrayed as a kindly woman who baked cookies, darned her husband's socks, or mended his clothes after his arduous journey around the world. Other stories have portrayed Mrs. Claus as the manager of her husband's headquarters at the North Pole, the person who oversees the production of gifts at Santa's toy factory. This is a far more feminist and modern Mrs. Claus than is usually depicted in literature, but is certainly an image that was picked up by certain producers of television programs and movies in the twentieth and twenty-first centuries. But where did the conventional picture of Mrs. Claus as a rather portly woman and homemaker come from? As it turns out, the origins of this image are not hard to trace.

In 1849, Christian missionary James Rees wrote a story that many believe to be the origin of the modern Mrs. Claus. In Rees' story, Santa and Mrs. Claus are an elderly couple—weary travelers—who need lodging on Christmas Eve. They are given shelter for the night, and children in the home are elated the next morning when they find that the couple has left them gifts before departing. The story goes on to explain that the two old people are not Mr. and Mrs. Claus, but are in reality the homeowner's elder daughter and her husband, people who had disappeared years earlier. There is a strong parallel here between Santa and his wife seeking shelter on Christmas Eve and Mary and Joseph seeking shelter in a stable in Bethlehem on the first Christmas. Mary subsequently gives birth, or "delivers" the first Christmas gift ever given, namely her son. Given Rees' Christian background as a missionary, the parallel is almost certainly intentional.

In the years that followed, Mrs. Claus appeared in print and pictures in many literary and scholarly journals as well as popular magazines of the day. In the Yale Literary Magazine in 1851, Mrs. Claus is described as attending a Christmas party, while in 1854 she is holding a baby at an insane asylum in Utica, New York, where Santa is visiting patients and children. She is also described in Harper's Magazine, The Metropolites, and Good Housekeeping in 1862, 1864, and 1887 respectively. Although these magazines described her as wearing a bit more finery than we are accustomed to seeing on the venerable Mrs. Claus, she was generally pictured as an elderly woman with gray or white hair and someone who wore a scarf, bonnet, or red hat upon her head. She was always dressed in skirts and dresses, sometimes wearing layers of fabric ballooning about her waist and almost always red in color. In many of these drawings and stories, she is standing next to Santa, although in a majority of them she is the main figure and topic of the work of art, with Santa merely a background figure.

One of the more specific references to Mrs. Claus and her duties appeared in the book Lill's Travels to Santa Claus Land and Other Stories, published in 1878. This is a charming story of a little girl named Lill who wanders beyond the confines of her family's orchard and discovers a wall that extends far into the sky. She travels along this wall until she stumbles into Santa Claus Land, ostensibly somewhere near the North Pole (or perhaps in an otherworldly region), and finds Mr. and Mrs. Claus hard at work. Santa is peering through a telescope as he watches children to see who is being naughty and who is being nice. Occasionally, he relates various details to his wife Mrs. Claus, who sits at a golden desk recording her husband's observations in the official "naughty and nice book." She is, for all intents and purposes, Santa's secretary. The book was authored by Ellis Towne, Sophie May, and Ella Farman.

We see a more proactive Mrs. Claus in an 1889 poem by Katherine Lee Bates titled "Goody Santa Claus on a Sleigh Ride." The term 'goody" in English and American parlance of the eighteenth and nineteenth centuries meant "wife." In the poem, Goody Claus gently pokes fun at her husband for her not getting more credit for all the hard work she does since Santa is the recipient of all the praise in the yearly stories of his Christmas Eve ride. She eventually convinces Mr. Claus to allow her to ride with him on Christmas Eve, and she slides down chimneys with Santa, after which she mends the socks of poor children that are hung by the fireplace so that Santa may place goodies inside of them.

In some twentieth century folk tales, Mrs. Claus takes on the sole role as gift-giver because Santa is ill and laid up in bed. She therefore dresses in her husband's red suit and stuffs it with pillows before driving the sleigh around the world. In some versions of this tale, she delivers the wrong presents to some households but trusts that everyone will nevertheless be pleased when they awaken on Christmas morning. The chief story illustrating this proactive role was the 1914 one-act play Mrs. Santa Claus, Militant by Bell Elliot Palmer.

Today, Mrs. Claus is seen as someone who plays an integral part in the Christmas story as it pertains to her husband. She is often seen at the North Pole, sitting in a cozy home, but movies such as The Polar Express, The Santa Claus, and Fred Claus show her and the elves as living in a virtual city with dozens of brick buildings housing the elves, Santa's numerous toy factories, and his dwelling. In many modern tales (as was the case in older stories), Mrs. Claus also has a prominent role as overseer of the toy production operation, and many scholarly observers feel that this modernization of Mrs. Claus stems from today's overt feminism, thus ensuring that Mrs. Claus is not seen as subservient to her husband but rather as equal regarding the tasks that he performs. In fact, in some films Mrs. Claus is black and much younger than Santa. A few movies have even portrayed her as a young housewife and not an elderly woman at all. She is sometimes a beautiful young woman who must live with her husband, a much younger Santa, who has somehow inherited the duty from his ancestors. Even Santa himself is seen in some stories and films as dressing in twentieth century attire in the off-season, meaning the eleven months when his focus is not entirely on Christmas. Mrs. Claus, of course, also shows up in most holiday cartoons about Santa and the Christmas season. It is a foregone conclusion that she is a real character with whom Santa could not carry out his duties.

Finally, the 1996 movie Mrs. Claus, starring Angela Lansbury, shows Mrs. Claus taking the sleigh herself on Christmas Eve because Santa won't consider taking an alternate, time-saving route around the world. When the reindeer Cupid becomes injured, she is forced to make an emergency landing in New York City. She calls herself Mrs. North and lives with a family of Jewish immigrants while helping the poor and needy of the city.

However she got her start, Mrs. Claus is indeed Santa's chief helper (and sometimes equal) and a figure who cannot be separated from the legend of Santa Claus himself.

CHAPTER TWELVE
Santa's Other Helpers

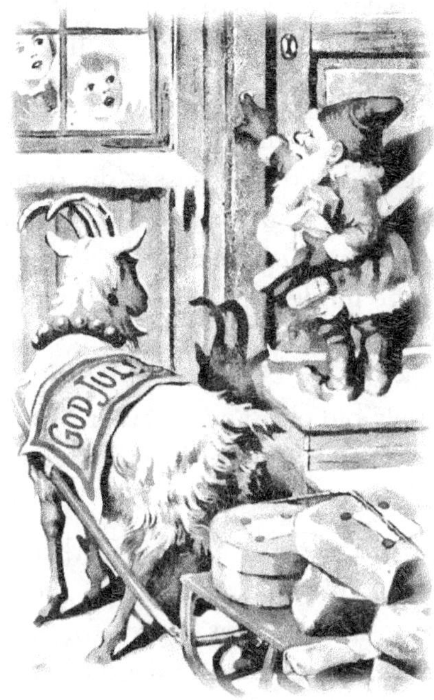

Everyone knows that Santa is aided in his workshop by kindly beings known as elves, although in some European and Scandinavian countries he is aided by mischievous gnomes and dwarves. In still other countries, his helpers are invisible spirits or angels who are remnants of pagan mythology. Whoever they are, they help make sure that Christmas goes off without a hitch.

There are many different legends when it comes to who assists Santa, both at his home at the North Pole and on his trip around the world on Christmas Eve. Exactly who accompanies Santa or helps him in any way has a considerable bearing on how Santa is regarded and depicted in art and literature. Most of the time he flies solo, but in many countries he is accompanied by helpers who are relatively unknown in the United States.

Perhaps the best-known helpers of Santa (after Mrs. Claus, of course) are his elves, which are often depicted in either red or green velvet clothing, and with caps much like Santa's. They are drawn as if they are dwarves and are mostly relegated to Santa's workshop as kind, hard-working beings who help make toys. But exactly what is an elf?

Elves originated in Germanic folklore and were described in German and Norse tales as beings with magical powers. While they could be impish and cause trouble for humans, most elves were seen as wise beings who used their gifts for the good of mankind. They were originally drawn as tall, slender beings (taller than humans, in fact) who wore green pointed woodsman hats. This generally describes the kind of elves encountered in J.R.R. Tolkien's trilogy Lord of the Rings. Shakespeare used the terms "elf" and "fairy" interchangeably, as seen in A Midsummer Night's Dream. In this respect, Shakespeare was using the term "elf" to signify small, mischievous beings (their mischief was mostly related to matchmaking) who were sometimes invisible or who could appear and disappear at will. The mythology of elves was quite diverse as the original Germanic legends spread from country to country and became conflated with different folklore in much the same way that the image of Santa was transformed or modified as it passed from culture to culture.

The notion of Christmas elves probably began in Scandinavia, where the mythology of the Germanic elf merged with the nesse (or tomte) that we discussed in chapter eight, with a nesse being a dwarf or gnome who was short and usually sported a long white beard and wore a floppy cap on his head. This is much closer to the modern picture we summon in our minds when we say "elf" in referring to the diminutive beings who live at the North Pole. In Clement Moore's 1823 A Visit from St. Nicholas, Santa himself is referred to as a "right jolly old elf," and whether Moore envisioned Santa Claus as part of this mythical species or whether he was using poetic license in his description of Santa is unknown.

But how did the Scandinavian portrayal of elves end up being Christmas elves—short, slim creatures who were relatively benign and had specific duties at the North Pole? The answer is that their part was written for them in popular American literature. Author Louisa May Alcott introduced the creatures in a book especially about elves, and they bore a great deal of resemblance to the folklore surrounding Saint Nicholas, Sinterklaas, and Father Christmas, a further testament to how all of these traditions had come together to shape a more centralized person called Santa Claus. Alcott's book, called Christmas Elves and published in 1855, marks the beginning of the modern Christmas myths about elves. although Alcott's tale (and poems that she wrote on the subject) still portrayed them as more fairy-like, and some of their duties included traveling with Santa and filling the stockings left out by children. Nevertheless, Alcott had yoked the idea of elves to Santa and the Christmas season, and that was a very large step away from the original German or Scandinavian concepts of elves, which usually had nothing to do with Christmas except in Norway or parts of Scandinavia.

The more common visual we now have of elves almost certainly stemmed from two more publications. In 1873, an illustration of elves working in Santa's workshop was featured on the cover of the women's magazine Godey's Lady Book. Similarly, the same visuals for elves were conveyed by The House of Santa Claus: A Christmas Fairy Show for Sunday Schools by Austin Thompson in 1876. In Chris Van Allsburg's classic The Polar Express (both the children's book and the movie), elves are seen much as they have been since the early part of the twentieth century, and the same can be said for their depiction in Santa's workshop in numerous Disney cartoons.

The elves' duties are fairly well known. They primarily help Santa make toys, although they also feed the reindeer, maintain Santa's sleigh, load his sack with toys in the days leading up to Christmas Eve, and make sure that the village where Santa lives remains hidden from the world. In some legends, elves maintain the naughty and nice list, although as we have already seen, many stories relegate this duty to Mrs. Claus.

But just how many elves does Santa have at the North Pole? In various legends that grew up about their lives with Santa, the number grew from six to nine to thirteen. Santa's headquarters at the North Pole, however, is sometimes considered to be an industrial complex, a small town with dozens of brick buildings, dormitories, and factories, with the number of elves is in the thousands. Elves are also featured in hundreds of Hollywood films about Santa and his home at the North Pole. For over a century, they have been a part of the legend of Santa and probably will remain so, with their role being integral to the modern American image of Santa, his wife, and workshop.

CHAPTER THIRTEEN
The Dark Helpers

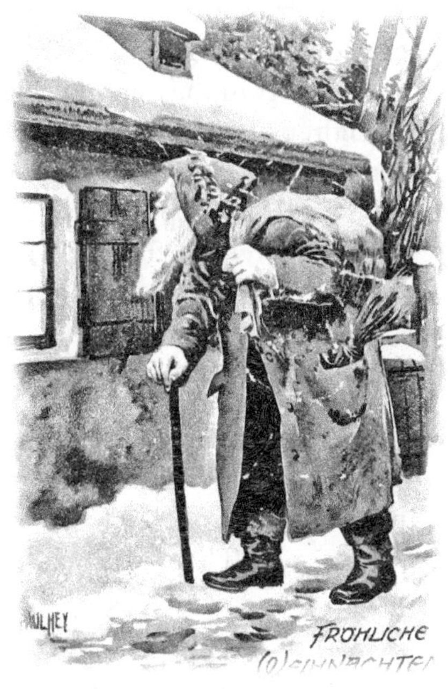

Black Pete, Krampus, Knecht Ruprecht, and Belsnickel are not household names, but these are the main helpers of Santa in most European countries. They are quite scary, however, and dress in dark, sooty clothes. Their main job was originally to punish naughty children and give them lumps of coal.

Mrs. Claus and the elves are the more well-known helpers of Saint Nick, but in centuries past, the helpers of Father Christmas, Saint Nicholas, Grandfather Frost, and other versions of Bishop Nicholas looked quite different from anything we can imagine today. As we've seen so many times in this book, much of the folklore surrounding Santa Claus derives from the legends and mythologies of various countries. In some cases, the helpers we're going to focus on were originally believed to be not helpers at all, but the primary gift-givers. Regardless, these figures were almost all dark and foreboding—not kindly or beneficent like the elves—and seemed to have originated in Germany and Eastern Europe.

One of the more well-known helpers of Santa Claus in Europe is called Knecht Ruprecht, which in English is rendered as Farmhand Rupert. He was originally the devil in German folklore, although Grimm's Fairy Tales associates the man with Christmas. Grimm, however, conceived him more as an elf along the lines of Robin Goodfellow, also known as Puck in Shakespeare's A Midsummer Night's Dream. Ruprecht was allegedly the primary helper of Saint Nicholas and has a long white beard, wears a dark, fur-lined garment and cloak, carries a staff, and has bells on his clothes. Sometimes he is drawn as having a dark face because he slides down the chimney with Saint Nicholas while delivering presents.

Knecht Ruprecht was, from his inception, someone who asked

children whether or not they had been good during the year and whether or not they had remembered to say their prayers, this being a familiar tie-in to the Christian theme of the holiday. If the children answered in the affirmative, they were given candy and sweets from Rupert. If the children answered in the negative, they received a switch or piece of coal, sometimes in their shoes, as a reminder to do better in the coming year. In other versions of this servant to Santa, children would be required by the helper to perform at the doorway of their homes. They were expected to sing songs or perform tricks, and the success of their performances was the indicator as to what kind of gift they would receive from Knecht Ruprecht.

*   *   *

Krampus is another one of Saint Nick's helpers who is prominent in Eastern European folklore. Like Knecht Ruprecht, Krampus is someone who, in most accounts in which he is featured, visits children in their homes on December 5th and demands that children either perform for him or account for their behavior during the past year. They are rewarded with gifts of nuts and fruits or else receive a switch or even a beating.

The origins of this character are unclear. Like so many traditions associated with Christmas, it is believed that Krampus, who is depicted as a dark, demonic figure with a devil's horns, is almost surely a pagan carryover into the Christmas traditions of Europe and became the helper of Saint Nicholas because he was known in his earlier incarnations as a demonic spirit who would usually punish children. In pagan legends, he was allegedly someone who could do great harm, but this is yet another example of how a pagan figure can be assimilated into Christian culture, even if somewhat imperfectly. It should be remembered that most, if not all, of these characters, including those of Saint Nicholas himself, are the result of longstanding oral traditions, meaning that the stories were passed from generation to generation, not by written texts (although this is the case in later centuries when writing and printing were more common in Europe), but by families telling their children tales over meals or a campfire, tales that were originally given to them by their parents and grandparents. As tales were passed down, there was a certain amount of degradation when it came to the accuracy of the material, and often the original sources were embellished.

The figure of Krampus was aligned with the devil or other evil spirits in pre-Christian Alpine traditions, and this dark figure was often featured in pagan festivals and parades. Although his figure slowly began to resemble a human being over the centuries, he was originally seen as a male figure with cloven hooves and the horns of a goat. He was decidedly evil and would often wrap children in chains in order to haul them off to hell or throw them in a cart or wagon and take them to the underworld. As can be seen, this is a far more severe helper of Saint Nicholas than someone like Knecht Ruprecht, and yet even today the figure of Krampus is part of Christmas traditions in Eastern Europe, the Balkans, and Slavic countries. Furthermore, it is believed that the myth of Krampus may have originated from the festival of Krampusnacht, a night on which he appeared in the streets to wreak mischief and havoc. (This festival still takes place on December 5th, the day before the Feast of Saint Nicholas.) He would appear alongside Nicholas (dressed in his bishop's robes and carrying a golden staff), although sometimes Krampus would stalk the streets alone. On Krampusnacht, Saint Nicholas only addresses good boys and girls, while the dark, hairy devil known as Krampus deals with the naughty children, giving them coal or Rute, which is a bundle of birch switches. His image has been toned down a bit since the mid-twentieth century, but he is still a foreboding, dark figure who does the unpleasant work on behalf of Saint Nicholas.

*   *   *

Another dark helper of Santa is Belsnickel, a figure prominent in Southwestern Germany, especially in the villages that lie along the Rhine River. Because of nineteenth century immigration to the United States, he is also a Christmas figure in Pennsylvania Dutch country as well as in Indiana. He is a thoroughly disagreeable and frightening character who wears dirty, tattered clothes, usually very dark or black, and because his flowing robe resembles a dress, he is sometimes referred to as Christmas Woman. He also wears a scary mask with a long tongue, usually bright red, protruding from the mouth portion of the disguise. In this respect, he bears a certain resemblance to Krampus and his devil-like appearance. This particular helper probably evolved as a variation of Knecht Rurpecht given his physical appearance and his overall Christmas Eve mission, which is to reward good children with fruit, candy, nuts, and cake while administering a beating with a switch to the naughty children he encounters.

The difference between Krampus and Belsnickel is that the latter figure does not accompany Saint Nicholas. In the southwestern regions of Germany, he travels by himself and is another Santa substitute. A variation on the spelling of his name is Krishinkle, which in some areas was called Krish Krinkle, and we again see another way in which the name Kris Kringle was born. There is no relation between Belsnickel and Christkindl, both giving birth to the name Kris Kringle, but the German language, one of the most complex of all European languages in terms of spelling and syntax, was fluid enough to produce the popular name of Kris Kringle via two different etymological pathways.

In Southwestern Germany and Pennsylvania Dutch country, a custom called Belsnickling occurs on December 5th, the eve of the Feast of Saint Nicholas. This tradition consists of young men dressed in bizarre costumes emulating Belsnickel—they wear masks, chains, fur, animal skins, or black garb—as they run through the streets of towns and rattle chains or bells to scare people, although it was (and is) performed in a spirit of fun rather than a genuine attempt to frighten children. The tradition also took hold in parts of Canada, mainly Newfoundland and Novia Scotia, and the custom is sometimes associated with the Canadian tradition of mummering, during which men go from house to house to perform and ask for presents.

In modern times, Belsnickel survives in both movie and print. He is the main character in the Netflix film The Christmas Chronicles 2 in which Belsnickel tries to disrupt Christmas celebrations. In 2000, a children's book titled A Pennsylvania Dutch Night Before Christmas by Chet Williamson featured Belsnickel. The book is a parody of Clement Moore's The Night Before Christmas and describes the antics of the mischievous Belsnickel as he travels on a plow pulled by cattle. The plow and cattle are so heavy that he falls through a farmer's roof when he descends upon the home to deliver presents for the children within.

*   *   *

Zwarte Piet, or Black Pete, is the chief helper of Sinterklaas in the Netherlands (sometimes called Holland), Belgium, and Luxembourg. Black Pete wears colorful Renaissance attire—rich robes and doublets—but appears in blackface and wears caps or wigs. The earliest depiction of Black Pete was in a book titled Saint Nicholas and His Helper, written by

Jan Schenkman in 1850 and published in Amsterdam. The story portrayed him as a black Moor from Spain, much like Shakespeare's character of Othello, a rich nobleman.

Black Pete is very similar to Knecht Ruprecht, Krampus, and Beslnickel. He rewards good children with candy and fruit while punishing bad children, sometimes whipping or even beating them. In some legends, Black Pete drags children back to Sinterklaas's workshop in Spain (and hence his similarity in appearance with the dark-skinned Moors of that country), where they must engage in slave labor by making toys and gifts.

But exactly how did these various dark helpers of Santa come to be equated with a blessed and holy man who brings gifts and the blessings of Christmas as a reflection of God's gift of Christ at the Nativity? The answer is that many medieval renderings of Saint Nicholas—in woodcuts, paintings, tapestries, and book illustrations—showed Saint Nicholas beating various pagan demons in order to defeat their evil powers. This is another example of how the celebration of Christmas was intended to replace the pagan rituals of the winter solstice, for in these medieval depictions Saint Nicholas defeats the forces of darkness and makes the older mythological figures submit to the new religion of Christianity.

If the above is indeed the case, then all of these dark helpers we have described are simply performing the same task as Saint Nicholas, which was to beat into submission those who refused to exhibit goodness and thereby honor the birth of Christ. Accordingly, Zwarte Piet delivers goodies, such as fruit (especially oranges and tangerines) to well-behaved children and, as always, punishes or inflicts some kind of corporal punishment on those who have not acted rightly over the past twelve months.

Today, in the twenty-first century, Black Pete has become politically incorrect in many cultures because the man who assumes the role of this Christmas character must wear blackface, especially when coupled with bright red lipstick and golden earrings. The character has been outlawed in many countries or is severely frowned upon. In other countries, Black Pete has been replaced by people with lighter skin tones. In fact, the actor's skin is occasionally painted gold to portray him as a friendly Christmas character dedicated to charity and good works. Ironically, if Black Pete's origins do at least partially come from the Moorish parts of Spain, where the population is primarily African in descent, then Black Pete is simply portraying a culturally appropriate figure plucked from traditions dating back centuries. Despite the controversy, however, Black Pete still makes his Christmas appearances in the Netherlands and surrounding countries.

*   *   *

Two more characters are worth a brief mention, although they do not represent widespread celebrations except in their own countries. In modern Russian folklore, Snegurochka is the the granddaughter and helper of Dred Moroz. She is also called The Snow Maiden and is featured in Russian fairy tales. The character of Snegurochka seems to have been born from a Russian folktale in which childless peasants named Ivan and Marya make a doll out of snow, with the doll subsequently coming to life. In some versions of the tale, she goes for a walk in the woods with other girls, who hop over a campfire. When Snegurochka attempts this, she melts and turns into a fairy or angelic spirit.

When the Soviet Union allowed Dred Moroz to once again function as a gift-giver, albeit at New Year's rather than the forbidden Christmas celebration, he was helped by his granddaughter Snegurochka, depicted as a comely young woman wearing a silver or blue gown, furry cap, or crown in the shape of a snowflake. The character is featured in a work by Russian composer Nicholai Rimsky-Korsakov, a piece called The Snow Maiden: A Spring Fairy Tale.

Finally, we have one more dark helper who still has life in some Christmas celebrations in Switzerland. He is Schmutzli, meaning "dirty," and he is much like the other dark helpers we have seen. He accompanies Samichlaus, and not surprisingly his function is to punish those children who have misbehaved. Dressed in tattered clothes and sporting a dark beard, he carries a broom, whip, or a bundle of sticks to chastise bad children. Often, he threatens to kidnap children, much as Black Pete does, if they do not mend their ways. Today, Scmutzlu's image has been rehabilitated, and he silently assists Samichlaus as he distributes an assortment of sweets to children.

PART FOUR
SANTA CLAUS IN MODERN TIMES

CHAPTER FOURTEEN
Santa Claus and the Coca-Cola Bottling Company

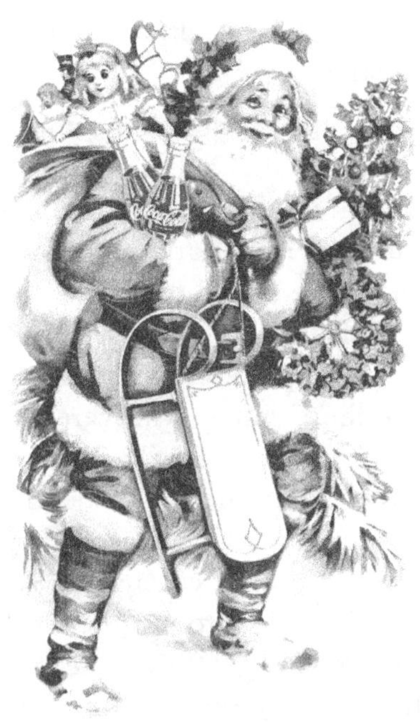

The Santa known by most of the world today comes from the paintings of Saint Nick commissioned by the Coca-Cola Bottling Company to promote its famous beverage during winter. Coca-Cola borrowed the image of Santa made famous by Clement Moore's poem *The Night Before Christmas*, and this image has become the most iconic in the world when it comes to Santa.

We have seen how the character of Santa evolved over a period of sixteen hundred years, beginning with Bishop Nicholas of Myra. The figure of Nicholas was adopted by numerous countries over the centuries, with each successive generation, according to existing traditions peculiar to a specific region, making Santa Claus into someone who fit their cultural norms, whether religious or pagan in origin. Hence, we see Bishop Nicholas becoming Saint Nicholas, Father Christmas, Sinterklaas, Samichlaus, Grandfather Frost, and the other characters already referred to. The one thing that unifies them all, however, is that he is a gift-giver, usually clothed in heavy red garments, who delivers presents on Christmas Eve. By the nineteenth century, Santa Claus had become a permanent fixture during the holiday season, a personification of the joy, happiness, and generous spirit of the season. The final incarnation of Santa, however, came when the Coca-Cola Bottling Company decided to capitalize on the jolly man from the North Pole in order to increase the sale of their beverage. It is their image of Santa that has become the standard for not only America but also for most countries around the world despite their regional portrayals of Saint Nick. But how did a beverage maker manage to crystalize the picture of Santa Claus in the minds of billions of people? It's quite a unique story.

The quandary for the Coca-Cola company was how to get consumers to drink Coke during the winter since sales usually slumped from October through March. How could they convince the buying public that their cola was not just a summer refreshment? Their solution was to link Santa Claus to the biggest holiday season of all, one that fell almost exactly in the dead of winter. It was, of course, Christmas.

The Coca-Cola Company decided to shape their advertising campaign around two sources. The first was the poem we've alluded to many times, that being Clement Moore's poem A Visit from St. Nicholas. In this poem, still read and celebrated today as the quintessential portrayal of what Santa does on Christmas Eve, we see all of the basics that have come to be associated with Santa Claus: he is a jolly man who drives a sleigh pulled by reindeer; he lands on the rooftops of homes and slides down chimneys; and he fills stockings (hung by the chimney with care) with small presents before leaving larger gifts around the family Christmas tree. The figure was iconic, and nearly everyone in the world identified with Santa in one form or another. This figure, Coca-Cola reasoned, was where they should plant their marketing flag. But what exactly did Santa look like? Why did so many versions of him exist around the world? Moore's poem had addressed his appearance to a large degree, specifying that he was dressed in sooty fur from head to foot, had a white beard, held a pipe clenched in his teeth, had eyes that twinkled, possessed rosy cheeks, and was chubby and plump.

This was a great start. It was, in fact, the only place to begin since this version of Santa had become fixed in the minds of children and adults ever since Moore's poem was published in 1823. But more was needed, and in advertising, image is everything. Coca-Cola needed to make the character even more specific while also creating a friendly image that people could relate to. In short, they needed to make their Santa more three dimensional.

The company commissioned Haddon Sundblom, a Dutch artist and illustrator, to bring the character to life in a more vivid way. Sundblom indeed used Moore's imagining of Santa as his template, but he wanted even more detail. He therefore turned to the Thomas Nast Civil War cartoon, discussed at the outset of this book, that had been published in 1863 in Harper's Weekly magazine. This original cartoon, however, was far too political since it showed Santa dressed in the stars and stripes and ready to punish Confederates. Fortunately for Sundblom, Nast had continued to draw pictures of Santa well into the 1880s, and they had evolved from year to year. By 1886, Nast had envisioned Santa much as Moore had described him, and he had even given him red coats and pants with white fur piping. This may or may not have been because Bishop Nicholas had originally been drawn many centuries earlier as wearing red ecclesiastical vestments, but regardless, the scheme would eventually work to the benefit of Coke since red was part of the cola's existing brand in terms of print and bottling labels (and much later, its cans, logos, and advertisements). The 1886 Nast Santa was a jolly round man who had a white beard, carried toys, smoked a pipe, had dimples and rosy cheeks, had a wide black belt, and grinned from ear to ear. Instead of a red cap, however, he wore a Christmas wreath about his head. This was definitely something Sundblom could work with, especially because the images were in the Public Domain, meaning that anyone could use them without committing copyright infringement.

But Santa still needed a specific face, one that would become emblazoned in the public's mind, so Sundblom was encouraged to get it right the first time. This was to be a Santa that would become lodged in the public psyche for decades, and it wouldn't do to have Santa's face change over time. This was a man who seemingly never aged, so he needed a face—and a good one. Sundblom decided to use the facial features of his friend Lou Prentiss, a retired salesman. Ironically, Sundblom cheated a little inasmuch as he started to use his own face as the model for Santa's features after Prentiss died, but the public barely noticed since the faces of the two men were similar, and given that the illustrator embellished the portrait of both Prentiss and himself, no one was the wiser.

That didn't mean that people weren't paying attention to the illustrations they saw in ads and in magazines. Indeed, they were looking at the illustrations so closely that one year they noticed that Santa wasn't wearing his wedding ring—an accidental omission on the part of Sundblom— and many wrote to Coca-Cola to ask what had happened to Mrs. Claus. In another illustration, Santa's belt buckle was backwards, and people wanted to know why Santa had changed his belt. The reason for this faux pas was that Sundblom painted his portrait while looking in a mirror, and on this particular year he had forgotten that mirror reflections always present a reversed image.

None of these minor hiccups deterred Sundblom, who kept tweaking his illustrations. In some pictures that he painted, Santa appears with children, and Sundblom used two neighbors, both young girls, as his models. He later arbitrarily changed one of the children to a boy. In 1964, he painted Santa with a gray poodle, the dog belonging to a nearby florist. This naturally caused people to think that Saint Nick was a pet lover. And why not? He often delivered puppies and kittens on his Christmas Eve journey.

Earlier, in 1942, Sundblom painted a "sprite boy" sitting on Santa's lap, and this tiny figure appeared in Coke advertising through the 1940s and 1950s. The figure was actually a depiction of a tiny elf, and as you might recall, our discussion of elves showed that these magical creatures actually started out as curious, ethereal beings not unlike diminutive angels who could appear and disappear. This 1942 painting further codified the fact that Santa was always aided by elves, and viewers of the ads usually assumed that Santa was at the North Pole when seen in the company of an elf. A postscript to this story is that the figure on Santa's lap in 1942 became so popular that Coca-Cola eventually named a new beverage after him, a drink called Sprite, which was a lemon-lime product meant to compete with 7 Up.

Advertising campaigns by Coke depicted Santa in many settings and poses over the decades, right up to the present. He can be seen drinking Coke, standing by chimneys, holding children on his lap, working at the North Pole, standing by vending machines and refrigerators stocked with Coke—even sitting in a chair and drinking a Coke while a small reindeer slumbers by his side.

In 1965, the Peanuts comic strip creator Charles Schultz, along with musician Lee Mendelson, offered to do an animated Christmas special for CBS, but the network turned them down. While the show, now a Christian tradition firmly established in the television lineup for the Christmas season, does not feature Santa Claus, it is another example of how the Coca-Cola Bottling Company has been able to influence the celebration of Christmas for over a hundred years. The show aired in December of 1965, and the TV commercials naturally featured Santa and Coke since the company was, after all, the show's sponsor. It was not deemed too commercial because the character of Linus recites the

Christmas story from the Gospel of Luke (at Schultz's insistence) and because Coca-Cola's Santa Claus was an integral part of the holiday season.

And lest there be any doubt, the company had more than succeeded in making Coke a winter drink, one in which sales spiked beyond belief as people stocked up on cola for their holiday parties. When one shopped at the grocery store (or any store, for that matter) in order to purchase Coke, it wasn't uncommon to see a life-sized cardboard Santa display in the soda aisle, and he was virtually the same Santa that people had seen all throughout the twentieth century in magazines and on television.

It is not an exaggeration to say that the Coca-Cola Bottling Company, with the aid of modern print, television, and digital media, took the most popular traditions discussed in this book and created what is now regarded as the definitive Santa, which includes his looks, home at the North Pole, his wife and helpers, and his yearly mission. This doesn't mean that the other customs we've touched on are not still practiced around the world, for they hold great importance in hundreds of countries. But suffice to say that with the world now connected by all forms of media, these regional customs exist side by side with the Coca-Cola Santa Claus. It seems that, thanks to Coca-Cola, this final incarnation of Bishop Nicholas of Myra, giver of gifts, is here to stay.

CHAPTER FIFTEEN
Santa in Movies and Films

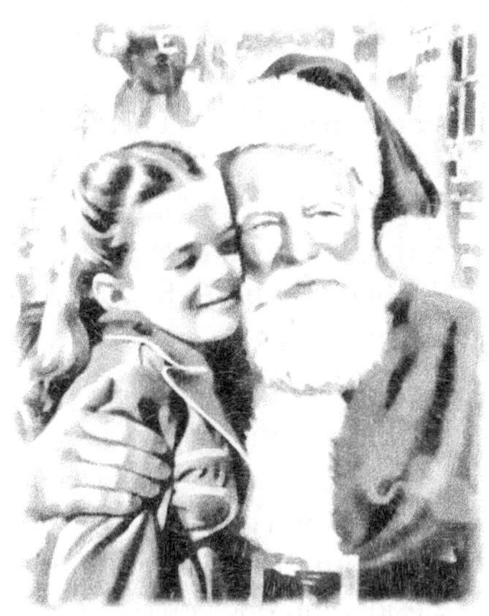

Santa's legend has been helped for decades by Hollywood thanks to movies such as Miracle on 34th Street, The Santa Claus, and The Polar Express. These movies have remained true to the legend of Santa even if they occasionally try to explore his origins and reality using a bit of creative storytelling.

Hundreds of movies have been made about Santa Claus since the invention of motion pictures. While we don't have time to consider all of them in order to show how the now-traditional image of Santa (essentially the one sponsored by Coca-Cola and the one in Clemet Moore's A Visit from St. Nicholas) has been bolstered by the film industry, it is worth noting at least a few of the more popular ones to illustrate how they have used the Santa described in the last chapter and further taken him mainstream to the viewing public.

One of the most popular Christmas movies of all time is the 1947 classic Miracle on 34th Street, featuring Maureen O'Hara, John Payne, Natalie Wood, and Edmund Gwen as Santa. As the story goes, a man calling himself Kris Kringle (the name for Santa, as we saw in previous chapters, that derives from various spellings of Germanic and Eastern European Santas) is incensed that the Santa who is to ride in the sleigh at the end of the Macy's Thanksgiving Day Parade—Macy's is located on 34th Street in New York City—is drunk. After taking the place of the intoxicated Santa, Kris lands the job as Macy's department store Santa Claus. His is a bit overweight and has white hair and a white beard, albeit one that is a bit more manicured than the longer beard normally seen on Santa in illustrations. As the movie progresses, Kris claims to be the real Santa, a claim that eventually lands him in court after a brief stay at Bellevue Psychiatric hospital. Previously, In Macy's cafeteria, a store employee accuses Kris of being mentally unstable, after which Kris hits the man with an umbrella, and hence his hospital stay and eventual appearance in court. Kris is ultimately exonerated and presumed to be the real Santa Claus when letters addressed to him and sent to the North Pole—actually landing in the Dead Letter section of the United States Post Office, which then and now really collects children's letters to Santa—are delivered to Kris in court. The argument made is that if a branch of the United States government, namely the Post Office, recognizes Kris as Santa by forwarding him the thousands of letters written to Santa, then he must indeed be the real deal. It is an ingenious plot that ends with Kris Kringle working magic for the little girl in the movie (played by a young Natalie Wood) by finding a beautiful suburban home for her family, which is what she had wished for.

The movie was very true to the image of Santa Claus that was emerging (again, thanks to Coca-Cola and A Visit from St. Nicholas during the twentieth century. No backstory was given for how or why Kris Kringle ended up in New York City, and what happens to him at the end is left to the viewer's imagination. But the lack of these specifics only reinforced the fact that Santa was a bit on the magical side, and one could not quite pin down his whereabouts or discover exactly how he did what he did. The movie was a huge success, winning three Academy Awards. More importantly, it further cemented the legend of Santa as America was about to enter the more sophisticated and media-oriented second half of the twentieth century. Through all of the turmoil of the sixties and beyond, the story of Santa remained intact thanks to films like Miracle on 34th Street.

Another Christmas class is The Santa Claus, starring Tim Allen. Allen plays a divorced man named Scott Calvin who kills the real Santa by accidentally knocking him off the roof. In the weeks that follow, Calvin and his son are transported to the North Pole in what Calvin at first perceives as a dream. Once there, Calvin is informed by an elf that the job has now fallen to him. Santa Clauses don't live forever, he is told, and every few decades someone must take his place. Over the ensuing months, Calvin begins to gain weight and grow a long white beard, gradually taking on more and more of the attributes of Saint Nick.

The producers of the 1994 box office hit claimed that, although they had indeed given the old myths about Santa a new twist, they had done their best to preserve the most important aspects of the legend in a movie that maintained Santa Claus was real. As they said at the time, the film posed no threat to any child's belief in Saint Nick.

The film tallies with facts dating back centuries, which is that Bishop Nicholas of Myra was, of course, not immortal. He died, but the tradition of giving gifts lived on in his parishioners and other clergy members, who carried on the custom of distributing gifts at Christmastime. As we've seen throughout this book, the tradition did indeed live on, and various figures replaced Saint Nicholas with each passing generation, an aspect that is reinforced in modern times by The Santa Claus. The producers may not have had this precise detail in mind when the movie was made, but it is in lockstep with everything that is historically accurate about the legend of Santa Claus.

Another class holiday film is The Polar Express, which was an expansion of the thirty-six-page children's picture book by Chris Van Allsburg. A young boy who is starting to doubt the reality of Santa Claus and the magic of Christmas is awakened to find that a train consisting of passenger cars pulled by a steam locomotive has stopped in front of his home on Christmas Eve. Without going into the many adventures that the boy experiences—all greatly enhanced and expanded to make the children's book into a full-length motion picture (live-action animated— the boy ends up at the North Pole. This is an example, as noted earlier, of how Santa's headquarters are sometimes pictures as an industrial complex of toy factories, living qurters for Santa, and elf dormitories—a small city for all intents and purposes.

Eventually, after more adventures, the boy finds himself with Santa on the sleigh, which is just about to head into the sky courtesy of the reindeer. A huge sack of toys sits behind them both. Before Santa can leave, however, he must fulfill a North Pole tradition, which is to hand out the first present of the Christmas season. This turns out to be a small bell, which he gives to the boy before flying away. The boy puts the bell in his pocket, but he loses it on the train ride home because there is a hole in his pants pocket. On Christmas morning, he finds the bell under the family Christmas tree together with a note from Santa, who found the bell and returned the first gift of Christmas to its rightful owner. The boy and his sister hear the tinkle of the ringing bell, but his parents do not since they no longer believe in Santa. Years pass, after which the boy's sister can no longer hear the bell either, but as a grown-up, the boy can clearly hear the ringing of the sleigh bell since, thanks to his adventures on the Polar express and his time at the North Pole, he still believes in Santa Claus.

Like The Santa Claus, this 2004 movie adds a new wrinkle to the legend of Santa while remaining completely faithful to the legend codified by Coca-Cola, A Visit from St. Nicholas, and a worldwide culture devoted to the belief in the existence of Santa Claus. Indeed, the entire point of the book and movie is to reinforce the reality of Santa, at least for those who choose to believe in Christmas magic and the tales handed down by generations of believers. That is exactly what we've seen throughout this book: traditions were handed down over centuries about a mythical, larger-than-life man who became the right jolly old elf in Clement Moore's poem. The movie expands on the myth without detracting from the slightest detail of the legend, and that's exactly what we've seen in every chapter on the origins of Santa Claus: variations that expand on a central theme while retaining the theme's core characteristics.

There are, of course, many other movies about Christmas that focus on Santa Claus. The most popular are Fred Claus, The Christmas Chronicles, Elf, Santa Claus: The Movie, Santa Claus Is Comin' to Town, A Christmas Story, Santa Baby, Klaus, Prancer, and dozens more. Most of the above movies (and others) do their best to be true to the most prominent aspects of the Santa Claus legend, meaning the contemporary (or American) Santa. There are variations, however, such as Santa Baby, in which Santa falls ill, leaving his gorgeous daughter (played by Jenny McCarthy) to don the red suit and fill in for him. She is more of a businesswoman who handles the corporate side of the North Pole, and she invariably falls in love with a handsome young man (catapulting this film into rom com territory), but even here we see a variation that is nevertheless founded on the modern traditions we have been describing, traditions that are an integral part of the modern American Santa Claus.

*   *   *

The legend of Santa is reinforced by the many Christmas songs that focus on the jolly man in red for their theme. The most obvious examples are "Santa Claus is Coming to Town," "Rudolph the Red-

Nosed Reindeer," "Santa Baby," "Here Comes Santa Claus," "Old Toy Trains," "I Believe in Father Christmas," "The Christmas Song," and hundreds of others.

"Rudolph the Red-Nosed Reindeer" and "Here Comes Santa Claus" were both written by film star and cowboy Gene Autrey. The first—"Rudolph"—naturally deals with Santa's use of a sleigh and reindeer, with Rudolph guiding the team on a particularly foggy Christmas Eve. Autrey's second Christmas classic—"Here Comes Santa Claus"—emphasizes Santa as the bringer of toys (again via sleigh and reindeer) but also makes pointed reference to the Christmas season as a time of peace, light, and hope thanks to the Lord, with Santa helping to usher in these traits by his philanthropic mission each year. In this respect, we see a distant echo of the many Santa Claus traditions discussed in earlier chapters that overtly connect Santa with the Christ Child and the Nativity.

"Santa Claus Is Coming to Town," first recorded in 1934, has for its theme the fact that Santa is about to make his yearly visit, necessitating that children need to behave themselves since Santa is making a list and checking it twice because he inherently knows who's been naughty and nice. This certainly reflects the many traditions of both Santa as well as his helpers, the latter being tasked, as we saw in the chapters on Santa's assistants, with rewarding or punishing children on the Feast of Saint Nicholas or on Christmas Eve. "Old Toy Trains" is a classic Christmas song written by pop singer Roger Miller in 1967. The lyrics talk about the need to get in bed and go to sleep because Santa is coming with a sack full of toys, and what could say "Christmas toy" better than a train set to circle the Christmas tree. It's an iconic scene that can be seen in thousands of movies and television commercials, and Christmas displays in store toy departments almost always have multiple electric trains circling miniature towns.

"I Believe in Father Christmas" is a different kind of seasonal song. It was recorded in 1975 by British rock group Emerson, Lake & Palmer. First, it is noteworthy because it uses the popular British term for Santa, namely Father Christmas. More notably, however, the song merges several strands of imagery to produce a Christmas song with many recognizable elements. It talks about a young boy who once believed in Father Christmas, one who looked excitedly to the skies on Christmas Eve, but also a young boy who heard about a "silent night" and peace on earth. As he grows up, he sees through "the disguise," this presumably referring to seeing a parent or substitute dressing up as Santa. The song remains popular, and many say it's a protest against the commercialization of Christmas. Greg Lake, the song's cowriter, claims that it is simply, as the final lyrics explicitly say, a wish for everyone to have a Merry Christmas. It is a unique song that encapsulates a dozen or more themes that still refer to the most recognizable elements of Christmastime and Santa Claus. All this having been said, the final line of the song states that for Christmas we get what we deserve. This may be a serious commentary on the presence, or lack thereof, of peace on earth. By the same token, the line, whatever its intended meaning, hearkens back to what we just reiterated, which is that children are rewarded or punished depending on how they behave. In this respect, "I Believe in Father Christmas" may well be a grown-up version of what we have discussed all along: Santa rewards people according to the way they live their lives, this reflecting the deeper meaning of Christmas since it is Christ, according to Christianity, who will do the very same for us in a much more serious context when we are judged after our death. However one wishes to interpret the song, the title perhaps says it all: I believe in Father Christmas.

If Coca-Cola advertising drew together hundreds of years of myth about the character of Santa Claus, modern film and music have only deepened the connection to this beloved Christmas figure by integrating him more widely into the culture. The roots of Santa Claus now extend sixteen hundred years into the past as well as into the pulse and rhythm of the season thanks to the artistic and commercial media that drives modern civilization. We are, after all, a consumer culture that feeds on all forms of media, such as radio, television, films, advertising, computers, books, poems, and art. Media, it is safe to say, is happy with the creative and artistic opportunities that Santa afford the film and music industries, which ensure that the Santa we have come to know remains alive.

CHAPTER SIXTEEN
Christmas and Santa Claus in the Twenty-First Century

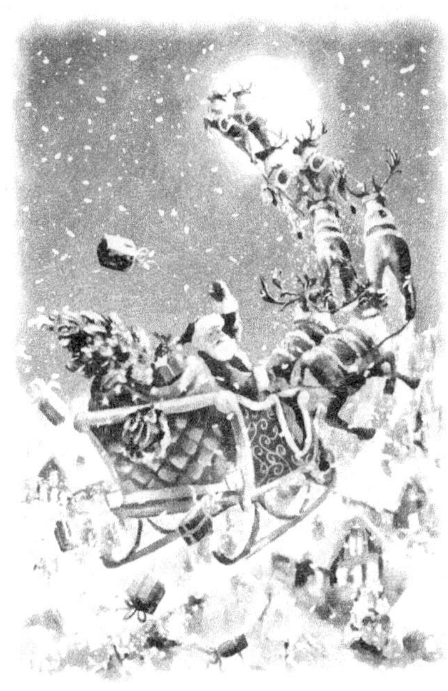

Millennials and Generation X also honor the tradition of Santa Claus. Despite smart phones and video games, parents still tell their children the story of a man who can travel the world in a single night to bring good things to everyone. It seems that no generation is immune to Santa's magic spell.

The two previous chapters have clearly demonstrated that Saint Nick is here to stay. He is part of the mindset of cultures across the world, but Christmas celebrations in general have evolved in past years, so what role does Santa play in the twenty-first century, a world that is increasingly controlled by the cultural norms of Generation X and millennials?

The answer is that Christmas itself has evolved much like the myth of Santa Claus (although one should be careful when applying the word "myth" to Santa given the real-life events of Bishop Nicholas and his successors, and we'll get to that issue in a moment). There's no doubt that Baby Boomers took the concept of Christmas and Santa viral thanks to modern media and suburban values—home, hearth, and family—that predominated American culture following World War II. Today, however, children grow up faster, confronting the realities of life at a much earlier age. With exceptions, most children today, by age five or six, learn that the magical Santa who can travel the world in a single night because of flying reindeer isn't real. And gone are the days when TV Christmas specials were part of television viewing beginning as early as December 1st. From the fifties through the eighties, variety shows, cartoons, sitcoms, and dramas usually devoted a single show to a Christmas-themed episode. That really doesn't happen anymore. Also, fewer department stores and radio stations play as much Christmas music as in the past.

Additionally, there are fewer Christmas tree lots in cities large and small, with artificial trees being the norm assuming families elect to decorate a tree at all. And even though Christmas season starts with a much bigger bang each year with Black Friday signaling what looks like a cattle stampede the very second Thanksgiving Day has passed on the calendar, many Boomers feel that something has been lost, that "something" being a special feeling in the air that caused people for decades to lower their guards for a few weeks and actually talk to strangers they passed on the street in order to wish them a Merry Christmas. Indeed, saying "Merry Christmas" has become politically incorrect in some segments of the population in favor of simply wishing people "Happy Holidays!"

In general, Christmas has become more and more secularized, with fewer people attending church during the year, resulting in the "once a year Christian" who might go to midnight mass on Christmas Eve. This, coupled with a generation of young kids walking around with their eyes focused on smart phones, has impacted the way we celebrate Christmas.

But to write off Christmas would be a big mistake, and it would not be an understatement to say that Santa Claus has played a major role in keeping the Christmas spirit alive in the twenty-first century. If only for the sake of tradition, millennials who get married and have children suddenly fall under the spell of a tale told to them many years earlier, and they have, by and large, elected to pass on the story of Saint Nicholas, read Clement Moore's poem, and turn on the television for their toddlers, rugrats, and kindergartners so that they can watch animated Christmas specials such as A Charlie Brown Christmas, Santa Claus Is Coming to Town, Frosty the Snowman, and Rudolph the Red-Nosed Reindeer. Kids also watch the movies we named in the previous chapter. And it must be remembered that Christmas decorations in the home and for the lawn are more popular than ever. Santa, of course, is one of the most popular figures to be seen on lawns starting in early December, when families string lights around their homes and adorn their property with decorations depicting the Nativity, the North Pole, snowmen, angels, sleighs, reindeer, candy canes, and, most of all, Santa Claus. It is not uncommon, in fact, to ride through neighborhoods and see Santa's sleigh landing on a manger housing the Christ Child. It may be kitschy, but Santa seems to be able to work his way into difficult places as much as he ever did.

But it doesn't stop there. Cities large and small decorate their business districts, street lamps, public parks, and other spaces with millions of lights as well as all the familiar figures and symbols of Christmas, and no figure takes precedence over Santa Claus. And let's not forget that it is Santa Claus, still riding his sleigh at the end of the Macy's Thanksgiving Day Parade, who officially opens the Christmas season.

As for music, carols are still played in stores and on the radio, even if they don't emanate from the speakers for as many weeks as they used to. The traditional tunes already alluded to are still played, and sometimes they include updated versions, such as the high-energy rendition of "Santa Claus Is Coming to Town" by Bruce Springsteen. When it comes to movies, the films we have summarized are still shown even though most networks have put a cap on the number of times they are broadcast each Christmas season. Kris Kringle still claims to be the real Santa on 34th Street, Tim Allen still morphs into the real Santa each year, and the Polar Express still makes a stop in front of a boy who is beginning to have his doubts about Santa. The exception to the curtailment of Christmas-themed movies is Netflix, which churns out dozens of Christmas movies every year, and the legend of Santa always seems to find a way into most of these films, even if obliquely by reference to him in the script's dialogue.

When it comes to more concrete decorations of Santa, one can find ceramic and fabric Santa Clauses three to six feet tall in CVS, Walmart, and hundreds of other stores, including those year-round Christmas stores already mentioned. Interestingly, he is sometimes portrayed as he was in the early twentieth century or, most astoundingly, as one of the European depictions of Saint Nicholas. In fact, many pricier stores sell entire sets of Santas that portray him as any one of the Santa figures we've discussed. Santa never goes out of style.

It's no wonder that Santa Claus has survived in the twenty-first century. Children may not believe in him as long as they used to, but their parents and society at large still imbue their minds with a figure that is compelling, one that is just too hard to resist—and one that sticks with them for a lifetime.

Or is this overstating the case? The question remains: how many people around the world still believe in Santa, whether as a young child or an adult, the latter retaining a begrudging belief in the figure into which they invested so much energy when they themselves were children. The answer may be found by returning to a real event described at the opening of this book. In 1897, an editorial penned by Francis Pharcellus Church titled "Is There a Santa Claus" was published in a New York newspaper, The Sun. In the editorial is the famous line "Yes, Virginia, there is a Santa Claus" because a young girl, Virginia O'Hanlon, had questioned her father as to whether such a man could possibly exist. Her father, Philip O'Hanlon, suggested she write the newspaper to receive an answer. Church's reply was eloquent in the extreme, claiming that as long as the spirit of love, giving, and generosity persisted, Santa Claus was most definitely alive even if inquiring people peered up chimneys every Christmas Eve and failed to glimpse the elusive Saint Nick. To paraphrase Church, he said that one might as well not believe in magic or fairies.

This is as good an answer as any that can be provided, and one, moreover, that has a ring of truth to it. For thousands of years, people before and after the birth of Christ have believed in a magical gift-giver who makes himself known at the time of the winter solstice. Thanks to Bishop Nicholas of Myra, he was Christianized and took many forms, but they all exhibited similar characteristics. Bishop Nicholas was real, and his kindness and generosity are a matter of historical record. Perhaps that is enough to settle the question. But just maybe Santa's existence is more a question of internal belief than external reality. Either way, as long as we have Saint Nicholas, Father Christmas, Sinterklaas, Samichlaus, Grandfather Frost, The Magi, the Christkindl, Kris Kringle, or just plain Santa Claus, the character is as real as we want him to be.

THE END